Praise for Power Trip

'McBride has a tremendous narrative gift, as well as great clarity of thought. The latter is a marvel.'
DOMINIC LAWSON, *SUNDAY TIMES*

'[I]t succeeds as a laddish manual of political thuggery conducted while at least twice the drink-drive limit.'
FRANCIS ELLIOTT, *THE TIMES*

'I've developed an unlikely crush on Damian McBride … His performance on *Newsnight* was masterly, reducing Paxo to platitudes. McBride's book *Power Trip* strips away the fluff, the verbiage, the feeble excuses and the patronising twaddle that gushes from our political leaders and their spin-doctors and we are left with the equivalent of cage fighting; *The Thick of It* now looks tame...'
JANET STREET PORTER, *INDEPENDENT ON SUNDAY*

'It is being billed as the "must-read" political book of the year.'
THE INDEPENDENT

'Current Affairs Book of the Year: This devastatingly forthright account of McBride's years as Gordon Brown's spin doctor and attack dog is the best book I have read all year.'
SIAN GRIFFITHS, *SUNDAY TIMES*

'McBride has now written unsparing yet defiant confessions of a "nasty bastard" – a detailed account of a powerful media manipulator at work, with advice on when lying works and honesty as a tool of deceit. It is pacy and McBride writes with a nice turn of phrase ... As a glimpse into the Brown bunker it offers much.'
ROBERT SHRIMSLEY, *FINANCIAL TIMES*

'[I]ts self-lacerating candour and humour deserve a wide audience. It is both a memoir and a manual, one that will serve historians, students of the craft of politics and – if they take the trouble to read it – those Conservatives who are even now working on how to get David Cameron back to Downing Street in 2015. It is the essential political book of the year ... His memoir will be read first for the elegant and lightly told vignettes. McBride can write, which makes it a pleasure to read...'
BENEDICT BROGAN, *DAILY TELEGRAPH*

'I have always admired McBride's writing – imagine Luca Brasi with a Cambridge degree – and am not surprised that his memoirs are proving so gripping, given the material and his genuine talent as a stylist.'
MATTHEW D'ANCONA, *DAILY TELEGRAPH*

'The most explosive – and expletive-laden – political book of the year. The memoir of Gordon Brown's former spin-doctor i~ ~~t f~~ *the faint of heart, but it contains some of* the year's most riveting prose and give   ›icians
would
DAN HO

'Best Pol
TOBY Y

'*Power Trip* is the political memoir of   ›own's
former spin-doctor – "McPoison" – he nas wrinen a racy, ~~~ ~~~, ~med
account of the last years of New Labour.'
ANDREW NEATHER, *EVENING STANDARD*

'A tale of treachery, dishonesty, expletives undeleted, and the subversion of elected governments by a talented rogue employee who was allowed to run rings round the system, largely unchecked.'
TIMES LITERARY SUPPLEMENT

'50 shades of Labour skulduggery'
PETER MCKAY, DAILY MAIL

'It is well written, generous to friend and foe alike and the author's undoubted boastfulness is tempered by heavy doses of self-deprecation.'
CHRIS MULLIN, THE NEW REVIEW

'Damian McBride is a bastard. And, unusually for a memoirist, he's very keen to let you know that from the start ... Power Trip is often as interesting for what it doesn't say as for what it does.'
HELEN LEWIS, NEW STATESMAN

'[A] very readable, and at times thoughtful, book ... Reading Power Trip, one is both fascinated and appalled by McBride's brutal philosophy, self-deception and pride in twisting the truth. What drives him from the first time he is asked to do some work for Brown is his love and admiration for this most unlovable politician.'
TOTAL POLITICS

'Westminster insiders and political reporters have gleefully digested the well-told tales in this long-awaited book.'
GUIDO FAWKES, THE SPECTATOR

'It is an eye-opener about the factionalism – and hate – that can exist within one government.'
ALISON PHILLIPS, DAILY MIRROR

'[Power Trip] reveals that McBride's notoriety was well deserved.'
THE WEEK

'It's worth [reading] for the insights McBride provides into the way we were governed during the New Labour years.'
CHOICE MAGAZINE

'For me the undisputed political book of the year has to be Power Trip - disgraced spin-doctor Damian McBride's occasionally terrifying account of his life and work in the court of Gordon Brown. He gives an achingly vivid account of his role in New Labour's palace intrigues in his confessional memoir, Power Trip. And he managed to shock even Westminster insiders who'd had an occasional glimpse of his activities ... [T]here are enough accounts of systemic leaking and brutal smears to provide a horribly revealing insight into the seamy side of political life. And it's very well written.'
MARK D'ARCY, BOOKTALK

'A cracking read'
LOCAL TRANSPORT TODAY

'This accessible account of the role of Gordon Brown's former spin-doctor Damian McBride provides an insight into many of the main players as well as the murky world of Westminster's journalistic goldfish bowl ... McBride has an interesting view on the Brown–Blair feud.'
PAUL DONOVAN, MORNING STAR

'This is probably the most enjoyable book you can read about that chapter of Britain's political history. Come to think of it, it's probably the most enjoyable book I've read all year.'
MILO YIANNOPOULOS, THE KERNEL

OMNIRAMBLES

OMNIRAMBLES

THE COLLECTED WRITINGS OF
DAMIAN
McBRIDE

Biteback Publishing

First published in Great Britain in 2014 by
Biteback Publishing Ltd
Westminster Tower
3 Albert Embankment
London SE1 7SP

ISBN 978-1-84954-789-5

10 9 8 7 6 5 4 3 2 1

A CIP catalogue record for this book is available from the British Library.

Set in Adobe Garamond Pro

Printed and bound in Great Britain by
CPI Group (UK) Ltd, Croydon CR0 4YY

MIX
Paper from
responsible sources
FSC® C020471

For Mum, 1937–2014

CONTENTS

CONTENTS

DON'T THROW THE BEER OUT
WITH THE BUCKFAST

16 FEBRUARY 2012

IMAGINE A WORLD where, like eating food in pill form, we consumed alcohol in 10ml shots of pure ethanol. Taxing that consumption would be simple: 50 pence per unit would keep the basic price high enough to discourage excessive consumption. And people sensible enough to dilute each shot with 90mls of water would pay 50 pence per 100mls of liquid consumed, compared to £5 for those drinking it neat. This is essentially the argument for a minimum unit price, delivered through excise duty: every unit is taxed the same and high-strength drinks are automatically taxed more.

In the real world, we choose to drink alcohol in a range of forms dictated by taste and fashion, rather than the need to ingest alcohol as purely and simply as possible. Brewers use huge amounts of water and grain to produce each pint of beer or lager: a 560ml product with only around 25ml of pure alcohol. Compared to a double measure of spirits, the ratio of production costs to pure alcohol delivered in a pint of beer or lager is exceptionally high. Wine falls somewhere in between.

Historically, the excise duty system has tried to recognise that variation in production costs. Beer is lower-taxed than wine, and both are lower-taxed than spirits – although gradually less so over the last decade. Once that principle of taxing each type of drink separately was accepted, other oddities crept in. Champagne has historically been low-taxed, as have fortified wines like port and sherry, again a recognition of higher production costs. Cider and perry are lowest-taxed of all (a bit of favouritism to home-grown products), while – since 2002 – beer produced by small brewers has been taxed at half the rate of other beer, a reform so far-sighted and successful that it surely merits an MBE – or at least a CAMRA award – for the official who designed it.

This alcohol duty system is far from perfect and the popularity of some cheap high-strength alcohol (Buckfast in Scotland – one of those low-taxed 'fortified wines' – and high-strength cider) can undoubtedly be laid at its door. The question is what is the alternative? The Institute for Public Policy Research (IPPR)'s Matt Cavanagh has proposed using the excise duty system to create a minimum unit price. While Matt debates where to set the rate, we can be absolutely clear about one thing: no government is going to reduce tax on spirits, so the assumption must be that the current rate of duty on a unit of spirits would form the basis of a minimum unit price for all alcohol.

So, compared to where we are now, the price of beer would have to rise sharply, ditto wine, and the price hikes for cider and fortified wines would be so steep there would be a real threat to those industries. But on top of all that, we would be handing a massive ongoing competitive advantage to the spirits industry over their brewing counterparts by taking the recognition of their different production costs out of the system. For a company like Diageo, which sells both types of product, the natural temptation would be to put their marketing resources into persuading consumers to switch from beer to spirits – something the anti-drinking lobby surely do not want to see.

The clamour for action on alcohol abuse is so loud at present, and the case for solutions like a minimum unit price put so persuasively by Matt and others, that there is a danger of the government rushing into legislation before thinking through the consequences. Pricing Buckfast off the streets of Glasgow is one thing, but surely not at the price of crippling the brewing sector, destroying the cider industry and, in the process, hastening the decline of the traditional pub.

McBride was responsible for alcohol duty in the Treasury between 1999 and 2002.

REMEMBERING THE
RIVIERA EARTHQUAKE

23 FEBRUARY 2012

ONE HUNDRED AND twenty-five years ago today, the French Riviera and adjacent Italian coast were struck by an earthquake which claimed more than 2,000 lives and created panic amongst most of the wealthy holiday-makers in Cannes and Nice. Most, but not all.

This was the record of the event made by the great Sir Richard Burton:

> A little before 6 a.m., on the finest of mornings, with the smooth-
> est of seas, the still sleeping world was aroused by a rumbling

and shaking as of a thousand express trains hissing and rolling along, and in a few minutes followed a shock, making the
hotel reel and wave.

The duration was about one minute. My wife said to me,
'Why, what sort of express train have they got on today?' It broke
on to us, up-heaving and making the earth undulate, and as it
came I said, 'By Jove! that is a good earthquake.'

She called out, 'All the people are rushing out into the garden
undressed; shall we go too?'

I said, 'No, my girl; you and I have been in too many earth-
quakes to show the white feather at our age.'

'All right,' she answered; and I turned round and went to
sleep again.

From The Romance of Isabel Lady Burton, *Vol. II, by Sir Richard Burton.*

JERRY LORDAN:
A 50TH ANNIVERSARY TRIBUTE

20 MARCH 2012

FIFTY YEARS AGO today, an instrumental named 'Wonderful Land' by The Shadows began eight weeks at No.1 in the UK charts. It was the biggest hit in the career of songwriter Jerry Lordan, an Old Boy of Finchley Catholic Grammar School.

Finchley has always had a strong musical tradition, and many talented artists have passed through its gates. However, none have had more impact on the world of modern music than Jerry, who attended the school in the 1940s and remained a faithful member of the Old Boys' Association throughout his life.

While enjoying a minor solo career of his own, it was as a

songwriter that he achieved greatness, writing Top 10 hits for Anthony Newley and Cliff Richard as well as The Shadows. Besides 'Wonderful Land', his other No. 1 composition – and the one that changed the world of music – was another instrumental called 'Apache', inspired by the 1954 Burt Lancaster film of the same name.

Jerry originally gave 'Apache' to guitarist Bert Weedon, but then picked it out backstage on a ukulele for The Shadows while touring with them in 1960. They recorded their own version and it became their first No. 1, spending five weeks at the top. It prompted cover versions all over the world, and became a staple of the Beatles' famous shows in Hamburg.

That might have been the end of the story, but in 1972, a record producer named Michael Viner decided to revive the song for a concept album by what he called his Incredible Bongo Band, reinterpreting classic tracks like 'Apache' with heavy use of 'breaks': percussion and drum solos within the main theme.

It was a low-key album release and, again, the story could have ended there, were it not for a young music fan in the Bronx named Clive Campbell. Campbell lived in a high-rise apartment block in Sedgwick Avenue. His large physique earned him the nickname Hercules, and when he starting DJing at 'block parties' in the apartment's recreation room, he dubbed himself 'Kool Herc'.

One summer night in 1973, Kool Herc tried a new DJ technique. Using two copies of the same vinyl record, he took the drum break – the part of the song that was best for dancing – and played it over and over again by switching from one record to the next, or did the same with breaks from two different records.

By using these breaks to create a new song, Kool Herc had taken the techniques of 'mixing' and 'sampling' to a new level. By shouting over the breaks with short rhymes or dance instructions, he popularised 'rapping'. And by encouraging the best dancers to perform in the breaks, he helped create 'breakdancing'.

However, it was not until 1975, when he started using the drum break from the Incredible Bongo Band's 'Apache', that his new type of music stopped being just the soundtrack to the best party in the Bronx and became a global phenomenon.

With his version of 'Apache' taking the Bronx by storm, the style invented by Kool Herc began to be copied by every DJ in New York, and record producers took note. A manufactured band – The Sugarhill Gang – recorded the first charting hip hop record ('Rapper's Delight') in 1979, and others quickly followed.

Helped by the release of the *Ultimate Breaks and Beats* series of compilation albums in 1986 (which included the Bongo 'Apache' break), sampling breaks and rapping over them went from being the preserve of DJs and record producers to something that any young person could do in their bedroom.

With the explosion of sampling, rap and hip hop continued to expand, and – with the annexation of traditional R&B in the 1990s by hip hop producers and artists – it has dominated the world of modern music for the last quarter of a century.

When Jerry Lordan picked out the 'Apache' tune on his ukulele in 1960, he could never have dreamed that it would one day trigger the popularity of a new DJ technique and sound that would go on to transform the world of music.

When he died of renal failure in July 1995 aged just sixty-one, the No. 1 single at the time was a hip hop song that dominated the dance floors that summer: The Outhere Brothers' 'Boom Boom Boom'.

Hip hop, rap, modern R&B and their various offshoots would undoubtedly have come into being even without Jerry Lordan, but the fact remains that when the histories of those musical genres are written, his name and his song will remain crucial elements. Jerry, we salute you.

WHERE GEORGE WENT WRONG

22 MARCH 2012

McBride posted this article at 4 a.m. on the night that George Osborne had delivered his 2012 Budget statement, which came to be known as the 'Omnishambles' Budget. This rapid diagnosis of Osborne's mistakes was highly influential with the media and MPs on all sides.

A T HALF-TIME IN last night's Arsenal game, I was talking to a pal about the Budget and – in the context of explaining where I thought George Osborne had gone wrong – I described how the Budget process works. He suggested I write a blog about it, so here goes.

STARTERS AND SCORECARDS

Bear with me while I explain some basics.

Anyone can come up with an idea for the Budget: members of the public who write in; NGOs and business groups; other government departments; officials in HMRC; Treasury staff, special advisers and ministers; and of course the Chancellor himself.

It would be nice to say they are all given equal weight and consideration, but the order I've put them in usually corresponds to the amount of effort the Treasury will put into developing their ideas.

Each viable idea – called a 'starter'– is given a snappy four- to five-word description – a useful discipline to check whether it can be explained in one sentence – and a lead official and lead minister are assigned to it.

It's also given a number, so if Chapter Six of the Budget is on the environment, each relevant idea is numbered Starter 601, 602 etc. With fuel duties etc., where there are lots of different options, they are listed out as 601a, 601b etc.

All the starters – about 150–200 in total – are placed in an Excel file called the Budget scorecard. Each line contains the name and number of the starter, and the amount in revenue that it will raise or cost in each of the next five years, before and after inflation.

Sheet One of the scorecard contains the starters which are almost certain to proceed, Sheet Two very likelies, Sheet Three probables, Sheet Four not likelies, and so on. Starters are gradually promoted to Sheet One over a three- to four-month process, and at the bottom of Sheet One – constantly evolving – is the Budget arithmetic, which says how much the entire package costs or raises.

No starter ever disappears from the scorecard. Even if it is firmly rejected early in the process, it still lurks on a distant sheet waiting to be recalled in case the distributional analysis of Sheet One calls for a measure targeted at a particular income group or segment of society.

On Budget Day, Sheet One is literally copied and pasted as a table into the chapter of the Red Book entitled 'The Budget Decisions', which is what politicians and journalists generally turn to first to see what the Chancellor's actually announced after he's announced it.

THE TWO EDS AND GORDON

So, what happens during those three to four months when starters are being considered for elevation to Sheet One? I can only speak for Gordon Brown's Treasury, in particular the two years when I was the official in charge of the scorecard.

Each week, with Ed Balls and Ed Miliband, we would go through the scorecard, line by line, sheet by sheet. James Bowler, until recently David Cameron's trusted PPS, would be there, as would Michael Ellam, the Treasury's then Head of Communications.

A dozen times or more, we would go over the same starter, and the two Eds would ask a dozen questions about each one. Why would we want to do this? Who's proposing it? How robust is this costing? What's the distributional impact? What does the minister think about it?

Occasionally, the lead officials for particular starters would file in for an interrogation, or the entire group would decamp to one of the ministers' offices to go through all the starters for which they were responsible.

In a separate weekly meeting, the two Eds and the ministers would then sit down with Gordon and repeat the process. Officials would be summoned for detailed discussion, additional analysis would be commissioned and digested, and, from those intense sessions, emails would emerge stating: 'The Chancellor has taken the following decisions…'

By that process, Sheet One would be finalised, and there is no doubt that – with a few painful exceptions – on each of the eleven occasions Gordon Brown stood up to announce his Budgets (twenty if counting Pre-Budget Reports), he did so confident that every decision had been comprehensively analysed and thought through.

As importantly, this allowed Gordon to dodge hundreds of bullets over the years – saying no to starters which officials and ministers had recommended to him, but which rightly failed to survive the intense scrutiny of the scorecard process.

ALISTAIR AND GEORGE

I don't know whether, how or why the process changed when Alistair Darling became Chancellor, but one thing was clear: starters that Gordon and the Eds had blocked on previous occasions began to appear in the final list of Budget decisions; officials had given them another whirl and succeeded.

One example springs to mind. There was a perennial starter in each of Gordon's last five Budgets to raise the road tax rate for older, high-emission cars to the much higher rate charged on their brand-new equivalents.

The DVLA proposed it every year for sound administrative reasons; DEFRA backed them up for sound environmental reasons. Gordon rejected it every year for the equally sound reasons that it was unfair and political madness to impose a retrospective tax hike on millions of family cars.

Alistair put the measure through in his first Budget, and promptly had to reverse it in the face of a media and public outcry, led by the *Telegraph*. What was telling was the reaction from Alistair's 'people': 'the officials didn't tell us'; 'we didn't realise'. Clearly, the scorecard process was no longer working.

By contrast, in George Osborne's first two Budgets, despite some unravelling of the North Sea windfall tax and the time bomb of the child benefit cuts, it was clear to me that the traditional scorecard process was working on overdrive.

I looked through the 2010 and 2011 Budget decisions tables, eager to see what fast ones my old civil service friends had managed to pull on the new Chancellor, and I was gravely disappointed.

These were highly disciplined Budgets where all but the most significant and carefully considered measures seemed to have been stripped out. I imagined George Osborne going even further than the two Eds in his scorecard meetings, rejecting without question any measure which did not fit within his big picture. I confess I was very impressed.

But now we come to yesterday. Even before the Budget documents had been published, even before I'd seen the Budget decisions table, I knew something was wrong when George Osborne said the dread words: 'We will also address some of the loopholes and anomalies in our VAT system.'

'For example, at present, soft drinks and sports drinks are charged VAT; sports nutrition drinks are not.' Blimey, I thought, that's Starter 328 from 2003 – Dawn Primarolo rejected that one before it even got to Ed Balls.

He continued with hot takeaway food. You're joking, I thought, not that old chestnut. I personally blocked that one back in 2005. 'Some companies', he went on, 'are using the VAT rules that exempt the rental of land to avoid tax.' That's hairdressers, I thought! Starter 318 every year. Gordon would never touch it.

Suddenly, I became worried for George Osborne. Where had the ruthless discipline of the previous two Budgets gone? If he'd let these kind of measures through the net, what else had he let through?

And what were his next words? 'We should also simplify the age-related allowances ... many pensioners don't understand them.'

CONCLUSION

I may be totally wrong. George and his team may have thought through every individual measure, and their cumulative impact on different groups, just as carefully before this Budget as they did before Budgets 2010 and 2011.

But for me, it felt as though they were so focused yesterday on the big-ticket tax cuts – 50 pence and the raising of the personal allowance – and what they thought were the most high-profile tax rises – fuel duty and stamp duty – that they took their eye off a number of other balls.

And it wasn't just pensioners. I'd be surprised if there were many Budgets from 1997 to 2007 when Gordon hiked duty on each of the six main excise duties: beer, wine, spirits, cigarettes, fuel and cars – because when he and the Eds looked at a scorecard with all those tax rises side by side, you can bet they would have frozen at least one to sweeten the overall pill.

The days after a Gordon Budget were often difficult as individual measures came under scrutiny, but it was rarely something he wasn't prepared for (the 75 pence pension being the obvious exception), and it rarely overshadowed the Budget package as a whole. The scorecard process had a lot to do with that, as well as ensuring there were a few (happy) surprises left to be announced on the day.

George and his team didn't seem prepared for the pensions row, and it certainly has overshadowed the overall package. Yes, that's because of problems with the policy. Yes, it's because the presentation was badly flawed. But also, and not to be underestimated, it looks as though something went very badly wrong in the scorecard process.

Someone didn't ask the basic questions the Eds used to ask, or they didn't ask them often enough. If they had, yesterday's Sheet One would have been much shorter, and with fewer unpleasant shocks.

THE EXAM BOARDS RACKET

3 APRIL 2012

McBride's first job after being sacked from 10 Downing Street was working in administration and teaching politics at his old school, Finchley Catholic High.

H AVING SPENT TWO of the last three years working in a top-performing comprehensive school, I've spent a fair amount of time listening to the gripes and groans of teachers about what was wrong with the education system.

Ministers interfering with the curriculum, OFSTED paperwork and health and safety bureaucracy were always high on the list. But one complaint stood out above all: 'bloody exam boards'.

The common view was that the exam boards were, to put it bluntly, running a racket.

As sole arbiters of what the exams cover and what represents a good essay or answer, they have a monopoly on what information and case studies students need to learn, and what practice questions and model answers they need to revise.

They use this monopoly to publish expensive, updated textbooks every year which no student or teacher can afford to be without (thus denying teachers the chance to recycle textbooks from one year group to the next), and they organise 'essential' and expensive revision conferences each exam season for students and for teachers.

Every time a new Education Minister seeks to adjust part of the curriculum to suit their own academic tastes, the exam boards happily go along with them because it offers a chance to print new versions of their textbooks, which schools feel obliged to buy and sell on to their students.

Then, when schools actually get to the exams and receive their results, comes the biggest racket of all: the exorbitant rates charged by exam boards to re-mark exams and coursework that they've marked harshly – or just wrongly – the first time round. Imagine a plumber leaving you with sludge coming out of your new shower, then charging you double to fix it.

And of course, driving all of this – the need to buy new textbooks and attend revision conferences, the impulse to get a re-mark to gain an extra grade – is the imperative for schools to keep up their place in the league tables, and for students to maximise their UCAS points.

So I imagine many teachers would have felt a rare moment of fondness towards Michael Gove this morning when they heard he was taking on the exam boards.

But if all he's proposing to do is hand their power and their monopoly to a select group of universities, what is he actually changing?

Won't it now just be the universities issuing the new, improved version of last year's textbook every September for £15 a pop?

Won't it be the universities holding revision conferences where – if you pay £200 – you'll get to meet the professor who's setting your exam so he can tell you how he likes essays written and drop some hints on this year's questions?

And won't it be the universities charging schools through the nose to re-mark exam scripts when a student's written the essay exactly the way the professor likes it and been given a D?

There's no easy answer to the exam board monopoly, but it's certainly not just transferring it to the universities. That may produce better exams, but it won't stop schools and students being leeched of money to make the grade.

FORTY DAYS IN THE DESERT
(FORTY-SIX, ACTUALLY)

8 APRIL 2012

Lent 2012 was McBride's first working for the Catholic overseas aid agency CAFOD.

I AM A BIG drinker. I enjoy it. I'm good at it. I drink far more than is good for my health, my finances or my relationships, but that's never stopped me having one more pint, on the grounds that there's no point worrying about one more after the first twelve. That's been the way of it since I was fourteen. Since then, the longest I've ever been without a drink was in

1998, when I was laid up following knee reconstruction surgery. After three dry weeks, I went out on crutches to watch a World Cup game, got drunk, fell over and tore the knee apart again. That might have taught me a lesson, but I blamed myself, not the drink, and rightly so.

During six years in political PR, I'll admit that – even by my stretched standards – the drinking got 'out of hand', as my normal evening consumption got combined almost every day with long lunches, quick pints and after-work receptions, not to mention the annual 18–30s holiday in suits that was party conference. I'd guess my consumption now is half what it was then, but that's still half of a big number, and I'd be lying if I said I'd cleaned up my act: when I was offered a six-figure salary last year to work in an Islamic country, my first question wasn't: 'Are they despots?' It was: 'What's the drinking situation?'

So when I told friends that I was going to give up booze this Lent, they were suitably sceptical. But working for CAFOD, where Lent is the focal point of the year for campaigning and fundraising, I was surrounded by people taking on extreme challenges – some walking the length of the Grand Union Canal or the Thames, several living for a week on seventy litres of water – and giving up booze hardly seemed a big deal in comparison.

So, after getting hammered for a week in mid-February like some dipsomaniac camel, I began my abstinence on Ash Wednesday. Forty-six days later, and for the benefit of any big drinkers thinking of embarking on similar challenges, this is what I've learnt:

1. Multiple motivations help.

   Much research has been done on the psychology of giving something up and sticking to it. I covered every angle: I read inspiring articles about the meaning of Lent; I made commitments to God and other divine beings; I got my friends to tell me I'd never manage it; and, as a good disciple of Adam Smith, I said I'd pay £1,000 to anyone who spotted me with a drink. On reflection, the one thing I should also have done was build towards some event or reward so I'd have felt excited in the last fortnight, rather than just limping to the line.

2. Home is a haven.

   My Lent commitment was made possible, or at least infinitely easier, by the fact that I'd already made and kept a New Year's resolution not to drink at home. So weekends or weekday evenings spent indoors were effectively temptation-free, something I exploited by getting myself addicted to new computer games and DVD box sets so I had a positive reason to stay in. I'm not saying I wouldn't have been able to give up external and domestic drinking all in one go, but staggering the two certainly worked.

3. Cravings pass quickly.

   Long ago, after my first hot summer day working (underage) on a building site, the foreman took me to the estate pub and I ordered a pint of lager. Since that day, I've always associated thirst and a hard day's work with beer, and it feels unnatural to deny myself that option on a weekday, let alone on the weekend. It took about ten days for that craving to pass, and while I continued to fancy a pint in various situations throughout the forty-six days, it stopped being my Pavlovian reaction to just being inside a pub.

4. Neil Tennant lied.
    There is no soft option. Now I understand why pregnant women look unhappy standing in crowded pubs: there are NO good soft drinks. The Fentiman range is great but sugary; ditto Coke and lemonade; pure fruit juice is too breakfasty; juice and soda too bland; and an evening on Diet Coke means a night spent awake. If I was Diageo, I'd market 600ml bottles of one part blackberry smoothie, three parts diet lemonade, and corner the huge 'no alcohol, no caffeine, low-cal, antioxidant, don't mind aspartame' pub market.

5. The belly abhors a vacuum.
    Danny Baker used to describe the 'lager diet' thus: 'Drink twelve pints a night for thirty years, then stop: the weight falls off you.' He has a point. There's a pronounced de-bloating effect, but in weight-loss terms, I found the removal of booze was almost entirely counteracted by a craving for high-calorie substitutes. Suddenly, I was discovering whole new aisles in Tesco: cream cakes, jam tarts, chocolate in all forms – anything for a sugar rush and the satisfied, stomach-slapping sense of having had a skinful. Not good.

6. Empty of beer; full of beans.

   I might not have lost weight, but the other physical benefits were indisputable. I slept deeply every night and, when I
   needed to, I could get by on very little. My energy levels were
   way up, and I felt generally buzzy all day. And as someone
   who is used to always having aches and pains, I had the rare
   experience of going several weeks without taking a Nurofen.
   I'm not sure where the cause and effect is with all that. Maybe
   the improved sleep produced all the other benefits, but they
   were there all the same.

7. Mentally, strange things happen.

8. I've been more efficient and methodical at work and, though
   usually a very nervous speaker, I've delivered presentations
   without the usual wobbles. On the flip side, my memory has
   been terrible: forgetting names, losing things, repeating myself.
   At pub quizzes, I've solved anagrams and worked out logical
   answers easily, but then been unable to dredge up basic facts.
   Why has being boozeless done that? It reminds me of when
   I forget my PIN number because I think about it instead of
   typing it instinctively.

9. Who needs a PIN number?

   I've saved a small fortune that would have been spent on
   booze. I've been putting that money aside and will donate it
   to CAFOD's Lent appeal. Indeed, thanks to the Department

for International Development and that nice Mr Mitchell match-funding all donations made during Lent, it will mean over £1,000 going to support CAFOD's water and sanitation projects. So lots of money which would have disappeared down my toilet will instead help build clean toilets for communities in Africa. Yes, sobriety hasn't made me any less trite.

10. Booze isn't everything.

11. Obviously, it's nice to know that I can quit drinking for six weeks if I need to, but would I have been able to stop indefinitely? This was almost put to the test when I realised Arsenal had won every match during Lent. Clearly, as long as that run continued, I couldn't jinx it by drinking, so I had to contemplate staying dry until May and possibly until the following season. Fortunately, QPR nipped that in the bud last weekend, but it's nice to know I was prepared to do it for the greater good. Next Lent, I'll try giving up Arsenal.

12. I love booze.

13. Given some of the benefits of the past forty-six days, it might be tempting to swear off the drink for good and become one of those dreary converted sinners. Well, sod that. I love booze and I always will. But that's precisely why I'm going to take it easier from now on. This Lent, I've experienced celebrating Arsenal beating Spurs 5–2 with a lime & soda and being

cooped up at home watching *Dexter* on St Patrick's Day. Neither was a great experience but at least they were by choice. I don't want to ever be told by a doctor or a loved one that I no longer have that choice.

14. So I'll have a few drinks this week but not too many, and then maybe another fortnight off. This time without the cream cakes.

RIP BILL HALPIN, 1929–2012

10 APRIL 2012

MY UNCLE, BILL Halpin, died at the end of March at the age of eighty-two at his nursing home in the Prime Minister's constituency. His memorial service was held yesterday in the presence of his wife Audrey and his large extended family.

Bill left school aged fourteen to work on the railways. Over a career of more than forty years, he worked his way up to become station master at Paddington and on many occasions he was in charge of the royal train, taking the Queen and her family on their official engagements around the country. As kids, we would sit enthralled by his stories of sharing Dundee cake with Her Majesty, and Prince Philip telling him off when the train arrived a minute early. On one occasion, he answered Princess Anne's remark that she hadn't slept well on the overnight to Scotland by saying, 'Oh, Ma'am, you should have sent for me.' He would still blush about that decades later.

After taking early retirement in the early 1980s, he took a new job that would have seemed extraordinary for anyone but Bill: helping Mozambique's Marxist FRELIMO government to build a railway to the coast so that it could trade freely with the world, something apartheid-era South Africa and its RENAMO guerrilla stooges were determined to stop. On arrival at his office in Maputo, Bill immediately replaced the photos on the walls of President Samora Machel and Fidel Castro with portraits of the Queen and Margaret Thatcher. When challenged by his new employers, he eventually conceded that the four leaders could adorn his walls together, surely the only office ever to see such a combination.

The job would have destroyed the soul of a lesser man: every time he got the railway up and running, RENAMO would bomb the tracks or derail individual trains, and he was back to square one, as well as having to deal with the terrible human cost of the drivers and guards killed in attacks. He spent as much time designing bazooka-resistant shields for the drivers' carriages as he did laying new track. He never stopped working, and even tried to soldier on through a bout of acute appendicitis rather than let a Russian surgeon operate on him, only conceding defeat after the 'bloody Commie' told him he was going to die.

If he was passionate about his work, it was as nothing to his devotion to his wife and his family, from taking my mother on his shoulders to her first Arsenal match, to the delight he took in the astounding and varied successes of his five children and umpteen grandchildren. And despite the demands of his immediate family, he always had time for his nephews and nieces: he remembered our favourite subjects at school; our football teams; and our best fielding positions at the cricket matches he'd arrange in his garden.

He was a wonderfully old-fashioned man. I remember him catching me with my lip starting to wobble at his younger brother's funeral, and telling me that I had a very important job for the day: to offer a strong arm to any of my female cousins who were getting tearful and upset. He also had that trait which I associate with old-fashioned Tories: a sense of duty to his employees and more generally to his fellow man – a duty to ensure that everyone was treated fairly and equally, and given an opportunity to get on. And above all, like all good uncles, he was a very funny man: an hour in his company would leave your face aching from laughter.

When I think about what is great about this country, I will always think of my uncle Bill: the respect for tradition; the insistence on fair play; the love of debate; the adventuring spirit; the obsession with cricket and football; and the sense of humour. I always wondered why he never had a MBE or an OBE. Of all the Queen's citizens during her long and distinguished reign, I can think of few who served this country or what it stands for better than him. Rest in peace, Uncle Bill.

A TRIP TO THE VETS

10 MAY 2012

TODAY'S COVERAGE ABOUT Andy Coulson's vetting prompts me to write a little blog about what developed vetting is, and why people have to go through it.

When I started my job as Head of Communications at the Treasury in 2003, every induction conversation ended up with me being asked: 'Have you been DV'd yet?'

'Not yet.'

'You've got to get that done.'

I soon found out why. Briefing sessions with the Chancellor ahead of international summits would be broken up as Gordon's PPS, Mark Bowman, said: 'Damian, you need to go out for a bit.'

This was especially frustrating for my colleagues if this happened in confined spaces, such as the royal flight en route to Brussels, where I couldn't 'go out for a bit', much as Gordon seemed to wish I could. It would have been impossible – and I mean impossible – to do the job I later did in 10 Downing Street if I'd been obliged to keep getting up and leaving the room every time something 'top secret' was discussed.

But at the Treasury, I was a bit baffled by the fuss. I'd been privy to Budget secrets for years, and – at Customs – I'd been present at planning sessions for major anti-drug-smuggling operations. Why did I need DV clearance now? There are two reasons:

1. Nothing quite prepares you for the eye-watering 'wow!' factor of some of the things you hear after you've been DV'd – they are top secret for a reason; and

2. If you're put into a high-profile role, you automatically become a person of interest for foreign security agencies, terrorist organisations etc., who may want to target you with honey-traps, financial blackmail, email hacking or anything else. So if your vulnerability to those attacks hasn't been thoroughly checked out, you remain the potential loose brick in the wall.

So, after a few weeks in the job, my time came. First, I had to fill in an enormous form – think a mortgage, passport and adoption application all in one, requesting everything from bank account details to your grandmother's maiden name. Why grandparents? So they can do background checks on your full extended family, and avoid the headline 'Olympic Security Chief Is Saddam's Cousin'.

I had to supply a handful of potential referees, at least one of whom would be interviewed either before or after my interview to check compatibility with my answers. And I was then asked who I wanted to do my interview: the choice was described as 'a kindly spinster aunt type who wishes you'd settle down and get married, or a retired sergeant-major type who thinks you're a poof.' I went for the spinster aunt.

When we sat down together, she looked over her half-rim glasses and said these chilling words:

> Now, I've done hundreds of these interviews, and this is your first one. My only task is to decide whether you can be trusted to tell the truth, so your only task here is to answer my questions honestly. If you do not, I won't give any indication, but I will write on your form that I cannot recommend you for clearance.[1]

With that jagged shard in my throat, we began. She started by skipping fairly quickly through the main 'risk' areas: sex and relationships; family and friends; booze and drugs; gambling and money. Based on my answers, she decided what to hone in on,

---

1 There is a legendary story in Whitehall circles of the high-flying young diplomat who was given this instruction and took it so literally he thought nothing of confessing his ongoing £500 a week cocaine habit. The story goes that his interviewer said: 'But you realise I can't approve you if you're currently taking drugs?' 'But I thought you just said to be honest?' said the diplomat. Clearance denied.

which in my case was sex, family and booze. The next three hours were by turns excruciating and exhausting.

Being unmarried, the first focus was less on fidelity and more on my history of sexual partners. She was testing susceptibility to honey-traps, how ready I was to bring strangers into my home, and where the risks lay of previous partners suddenly and suspiciously re-entering my life now I'd got this new job. She insisted on going through every bit of that history, from long-term relationships to one-night stands: names, locations, details, current status etc.

She then went on to probably the worst five minutes of my life: this kindly spinster aunt – exactly as billed – listing every sexual practice you can think of and asking if I'd ever engaged in them. I won't list her questions – this is a family blog – but my answers went something like: 'No… No… No… Erm, no… No… Yes, but only once… No… No… No… What is that? Oh, bloody hell – of course not…'

It was a great relief when she moved onto family, but I realised then that all the background checks had kicked up some concerns. 'Would you describe your father as an Irish nationalist?', 'What about his family?', 'How often do you travel to Donegal?', 'Do you meet your cousins there?', 'Have any of your cousins ever spoken to you about Irish nationalism?'

I knew what specifically she was driving at, and – rather than have it crushed out of me – I told her exactly what I knew about the seventeen members of my extended Irish family who regarded the modern IRA as murderers, thugs and criminals, and the one bad apple who differed.

After all that, booze was easy. Unlike a doctor, she couldn't care less how much I drank but just wanted to know where I drank, how loudly I talked, whether I took my briefcase with me, whether I ever lost things,[2] and most of all, could I remember how I behaved when actually drunk. My answers wouldn't have been totally reassuring but they were honest and – crucially – they were consistent with those my friend Anthony had given when she'd asked him that morning.

And that was it. She thanked me, I went away, and two weeks' later, I was told I'd been cleared. What would I conclude that is relevant to the Andy Coulson issue? Well, all I know is this: if I had lied to that kindly woman with the half-rim glasses, she'd have known it in a heartbeat – so I'd defy anyone to go through that process and come through with their secrets still hidden.

---

2 Coincidentally, the only time I did get drunk and lose any official papers, it was the mysterious application form I was sent by a specialist branch of government who were interested in inviting me to a further assessment process after I was accepted to the Fast Stream Civil Service in 1996. I called the number on the letter and asked them for a replacement form. They said they didn't know what I was talking about and hung up.

ERROL BARROW AND
THE MIRROR IMAGE

1 JUNE 2012

TWENTY-FIVE YEARS AGO today, one of my heroes, Errol Barrow, died at the age of sixty-seven. His was an incredible life. Born and educated in Barbados, he gave up his academic career aged twenty to join the RAF. He survived more than forty-five bombing missions over mainland Europe, rising to the rank of Flying Officer and serving on the private plane of future Air Marshal Sholto Douglas. He trained for the Bar in London, but returned to Barbados in 1950 to embark on a career in politics.

And what a career: founder of the Democratic Labour Party; Premier in 1961; and – after leading Barbados to peaceful independence

41

in 1966 – its first Prime Minister. His first period in office saw a raft of social and economic reforms, from funding free universal secondary education to masterminding economic cooperation and free trade between the Caribbean islands. He left office in 1976 and, after a period out of politics and away from Barbados, he returned, more radical than ever and a fierce critic of American influence in the region.

On 13 May 1986, two weeks before the general election, he stood on a DLP platform as candidate for Prime Minister, and delivered the 'mirror image' speech, one of the greatest of all political speeches. It is great not just because of the marvellous rhetorical technique, not just because of the easy mix of the homespun and the firebrand, and not even because of the hilarious ending ('Anyhow, ladies and gentlemen, I done').

For me, it is great most of all because it seems unimaginable that any politician of our age would have the courage and belief to make a speech essentially berating the people of his country, criticising their attitude and ambition, let alone do so two weeks before an election. And yet, he won a massive victory, the DLP winning all but three of the twenty-seven Assembly seats. He died just over a year later, but his legacy survives to this day.

Here are edited extracts from the 'mirror image' speech, 13 May 1986:

> What I wish to speak to you about very briefly here this evening is about you. About yourself.
>
> I want to know what kind of mirror image do you have of

yourself? Do you really like yourselves? There are too many people in Barbados who despise themselves, and their dislike of themselves reflects itself in their dislike of other people.

Now, what has bothered me in this society is that every time after elections, people expect certain things to take place. And although the law says that he that giveth is as much guilty of bribery and corruption under the Corrupt Practices Act as he that receiveth, we know that even on polling day, people were given envelopes with $100 bills in them.

So what kind of mirror image would you have of yourself? If there are corrupt ministers in Barbados tonight, you have made them corrupt.

I am not trying to make any excuses for you, but I realise what has happened in this society. I look around and see people who have not done an honest day's work in their whole lives driving around in MP cars, having an ostentatious standard of living, unlike my poor families in St John, who the welfare officer gives $50 to feed a family of ten for a whole week.

What kind of mirror image can you have of yourself?

You so much despair of this society that your greatest ambition is to try to prove to the people of the United States Consulate that you are only going up to visit your family [...] And you are surprised when the people at the United States embassy tell you that you do not have a strong reason to return to Barbados. And you are the only person dishonest enough with yourself to realise that you do not have a strong reason to return to Barbados, because Barbados has nothing to offer you. You are not being honest with yourself, but you tell the man down there, 'Oh yes, I'm returning.'

When I went to Mexico, I had to make a decision, and I returned. I had a strong reason. My reason is that I did not want to see my country go down the drain but you who are not in politics don't have a strong reason.

Your ambition in life is to try and get away from this country. And we call ourselves an independent nation? When all we want to do is go and scrub somebody's floors and run somebody's elevator or work in somebody's store or drive somebody's taxi in a country where you catching your royal when the winter sets in?

What kind of mirror image do you have of yourself? Let me tell you what kind of mirror image I have of you. The Democratic Labour Party has an image that the people of Barbados would be able to run their own affairs, to pay for the cost of running their own country, to have an education system which is as good as what can be attained in any industrialised country, anywhere in the world.

In the state of Texas, the government of that state has asked to make the teachers pass an examination. To see if they can read and write! The gentleman of the Texas teachers' union came on the news and he said that he was proud of the result because only 8 per cent of the teachers couldn't read and write!

If Reagan had to take the test, I wonder if he would pass. But this is the man that you all say how great he is for bombing the people in Libya and killing little children [...] This is the man that you all go up at the airport and put down a red carpet for, and he is the President of a country in which in one of the more advanced and biggest states 8 per cent of the teachers cannot read and write, and he feels that they are better than we. And you feel that we should run up there and bow.

What kind of mirror image do you have of yourself? When a government steals from people in the way of consumption taxes and takes that money and spends it on their own high lifestyles, and unnecessary buildings, then that government not only has contempt for you, but, what is most unfortunate, you have contempt for yourself, because you allow them to do it.

What kind of mirror image do you have of yourself when you allow the mothers of this nation to be beasts of burden in the sugarcane fields? In Mexico, where people suffer under a lower standard of living than in Barbados, they use donkeys to freight canes out of the fields; in Antigua, they use a small railway; but here the mothers of the nation are used as beasts of burden. What kind of image do you have of yourself?

I was inspired by the work done by the late Mr Ernest Bevin, who went to work at eight – I don't mean eight o'clock in the mornin', I mean eight years of age – and those dock workers in London used to turn up during the winter and summer from five o'clock in the morning waiting for a ship, and if a ship didn't come in for three weeks or three months, they wouldn't get any pay. And Ernest Bevin introduced the guaranteed week for dock workers. I set up a commission of inquiry into the sugar industry and made the examination of the guaranteed week for agricultural workers one of the terms of reference, and the commission reported that nobody gave any evidence before them in support of this recommendation.

What kind of mirror image do the people of the Workers' Union have, either of you or themselves? I had to wait until there was a dispute in the sugar industry and say, well, these will be the wages from next week and [...] I went into the House and introduced the guaranteed wages for agricultural workers. Why should only one man have a mirror image of you that you do not want to have of yourself? What kind of society are we striving for? There is no point in striving for Utopia, but you do not realise your potential.

I lived in a little country when I was young: the Virgin Islands. That is a small country. But there is another small country. That country has 210 square miles; it is 40 square miles bigger than Barbados. If you took the parish of St Philip and put it right in the little curve by Bathsheba, that would be the size of the country of Singapore.

But you know the difference between Barbados and that country? First, Barbados has 250,000 people. You know how many people Singapore has on 40 more square miles? Over two and a half million, on an island just a little larger than Barbados.

They don't have sugar plantations; they don't have enough land to plant more than a few orchids. They don't have enough land to plant a breadfruit tree in the backyard and nearly every Barbadian have some kind of fruit tree in the backyard.

They have developed an education system but they are teaching people things that are relevant to the twenty-first century.

They are not teaching people how to weed by the road. They are in the advance of the information age.

But you know the difference between you and them? They have got a mirror image of themselves. They are not looking to get on any plane to go to San Francisco. Too far away. The government does not encourage them to emigrate unless they are going to develop business for Singapore.

They have a mirror image of themselves. They have self-respect. They have a desire to move their country forward by their own devices. They are not waiting for anybody to come and give them handouts. And there is no unemployment.

Is that the mirror image that you have of yourselves?

Anyhow, ladies and gentlemen, I done.

FIVE YEARS ON:
THE DAY GB BECAME PM

27 JUNE 2012

FIVE YEARS AGO today, Gordon Brown became Prime Minister. Here are some personal memories and reflections…

It's not often you're paid to hurl abuse at someone who's about to become the most powerful man in the country, but that's how the day started. Sue Nye and I joined Gordon and Sarah in one of the large rooms on the Treasury's ministerial corridor, where he was rehearsing the speech he'd make outside No. 10. Given Iraq War protestors were already gathering at the Downing Street gates to see off Tony Blair, we suggested he do a few run-throughs with us heckling him so he could get used to the distraction he'd experience later. Sue's heckles were from the *Father Ted* school ('Booo!', 'Hiss!', 'You're a very bad man!' etc.), but I tried to get in the spirit a bit more: 'Blood on your hands, Brown!'; 'You're a murderer, Brown!'; 'Tell us about Bilderberg!' etc. Every so often, I'd shout something that would get under his skin, and he'd stop his speech and just give me a long, deathly stare. I'd protest: 'Well, you can't do that if someone says it in the street', which got me another stare. I did always wonder what any Treasury officials passing outside the room would have thought hearing Gordon booming out 'I will do my utmost' while I shouted back at him, 'Sod off, you Scottish git!'

Given Gordon's reputation as a hard taskmaster, you might think Treasury officials were happy to see the back of him, but the mood that day was sombre. Remember that the majority of the staff had only ever worked under Gordon, and the older officials had never known a time when the Treasury was more powerful and well-drilled. The connection was personal too: these were staff who had openly wept when Gordon's daughter had died, and if he didn't know each of their names, he knew them by their functions ('SureStart Girl', 'Road Tax Guy'), or the football team they supported.[3] When Gordon was waiting for the summons to the palace, they silently gathered on the balconies and in the atrium to applaud him out, and I'd rarely seen him so moved. A great civil servant named David Martin – who'd worked in the

---

3 Over the space of ten years since I came to his attention working on the abolition of gambling tax, I went from being 'Betting Guy' to 'Fuel Guy' to 'That Guy McBride' to 'Bloody Celtic' to 'Dominic' to 'Damian' and finally to 'Mr McBride' (in interviews circa April 2009).

Treasury's Parliamentary Unit for decades – was asked at his retirement party in 2009 who his favourite Chancellor was. Without hesitation, he replied: 'Gordon.' Why? 'Because we knew what we were doing.' He recounted that, on the day of Gordon's departure, Nick Macpherson – the Treasury's top official – approached him and said, 'Right, we can go back to the way things used to be,' to which David replied: 'Why on earth would we want to do that?'

Gordon's welcome in No. 10 was understandably more muted than his farewell from the Treasury, but he won a lot of the staff round when he addressed them later that afternoon. He said he knew this was a day of great sadness for them, having to say goodbye to Tony, Cherie, Euan, Nicky, Catherine, and especially Leo, whom many of them had known since he was a baby, and that they'd also said goodbye to a great many friends amongst Tony's advisers who would be sorely missed.[4] It was a source of great angst for Gordon that he hadn't managed to persuade any of Tony's senior political advisers to stay on and support the succession. He went to frankly humiliating lengths to try to talk individuals like Catherine Rimmer into working for him, all in the name of demonstrating to diehard Blairites that he was willing to carry their flame. In retrospect, the effort to woo even junior members of the Blair circle in the weeks before his takeover was a vast waste of time. But arguably, if he'd succeeded, it would have strengthened

---

4 An interesting contrast to David Cameron, whose only reference to his two predecessors in his first speech to Downing Street staff was to joke that a civil servant had told him he and Nick Clegg were already getting on better than Blair and Brown, and he hoped to set the bar a bit higher than that.

his hand to make major departures from Blair policies in his early days. Proposals such as scrapping tuition fees, which had been high on the list of planned announcements, were shelved because Gordon didn't feel secure enough against a Blairite backlash.

While Gordon was settling in at No. 10, I was still in my Treasury office.[5] I wrote a good luck card to my successor, Alistair Darling's special adviser Sam White, and left it propped up against a bottle of whiskey on my desk. My moving crates were collected and I filled three bin bags with rubbish and old papers. I sat in my empty office flicking between Nick Robinson and Adam Boulton outside Downing Street, occasionally sending abusive texts to fellow Brown staffers milling aimlessly in the background telling them: 'Get out of the fucking shot.' Not because it spoiled the pictures, but I knew some of them were trying their best to be spotted on camera and in the process making us look like excited amateurs to our new No. 10 colleagues. I continued sitting alone in my office for hours, taking calls from hacks about everything from the impending reshuffle to what Gordon had eaten for breakfast. Eventually Sue called me: 'Where are you?' – not a question she was unused to asking.

'I'm still in the Treasury.'

'Well, you know you work here now, don't you?'

---

5 This office is now occupied by George Osborne's media adviser, Ramesh (Mesh) Chaabra, although I understand when he calls the Treasury press office, my name still pops up on their desk phones. It has been my tradition every year since 2005 to make one call to the press office on Budget Day pretending to be from a specialist journal and challenging some obscure Budget measure, just to check they are on their mettle. I left them alone this year … they had enough real calls to deal with.

After eleven years in the Treasury and Customs, my stomach was in knots about having to leave. And after all those years striving to make sure it was Gordon who took over from Tony in No. 10, I was terrified to go there myself. Eventually I left, in floods of tears.

There's no getting around the fact that, by this point, many of the No. 10 civil servants who'd worked under Tony regarded me with something between distrust and hatred, but they were totally professional when greeting me and on the surface very friendly. It helped that I was sat in an office with old Alastair Campbell acolytes Paul Brown and Martin Sheehan, two of the nicest chaps you could meet, and both brilliant at their jobs planning the government's grid of announcements and speeches. In hushed tones, I was shown the 'stand-alone computer' through which No. 10 staff could use personal email accounts which were otherwise blocked by the Downing Street servers. 'We don't discuss this publicly,' I was told. 'We don't want people going on about "second Downing Street email systems".' What I wasn't shown that day was the secret underground tunnel to the Whitehall nuclear bunker. It was only after a series of staff departures in 2008 that I was told I'd finally made it onto the list of key officials and advisers who would be bundled off to safety with the Cabinet when the bombs dropped. By that stage, I'm afraid my reaction was: 'Do I have to be?'

The other consequence of the mass exodus of the Blair family and advisers from No. 10 was the sheer volume of files, letters, lanyards, chipped mugs, stained ties and other detritus that had been piled up to go in the skip. I am an appalling hoarder and had a good root around in the rubbish to recover any serviceable books, stationery and so on. My prize find was Tony Blair's *GQ* Politician of the Year Award from September 2003, a lovely piece of slate and glass, which now sits in pride of place on my mantelpiece at home.

Late into the evening, there was a fairly exhausted gathering of long-term Brown staffers to watch the ten o'clock news and have a drink. It wasn't quite the 'Clair de Lune' scene at the end of *The Right Stuff,* but for those of us who'd been at Gordon's side for a while, the handshakes and hugs were full of pride and relief. Becoming Prime Minister is no easy thing. Only five people have achieved it in the last thirty-two years, only two of those (Thatcher and Blair) by winning elections outright. In that same period, perhaps a hundred other ambitious men and women have at some stage been tipped for the top job but come up short. The five who succeeded were all to some degree reliant on small groups of smart, committed, loyal people prepared to sweat every last drop of blood and sacrifice their own personal lives and ambitions to get them there. Many of the hundred who failed either lacked that support or thought they didn't need it. By rights, Gordon's chance of ever becoming Prime Minister should have disappeared in 1994. To survive thirteen years, ten of them in government, as the main contender – and consistently the public's favoured choice – to succeed Tony Blair was an astonishing feat of personal discipline and political resilience. And those of us who helped him achieve it rightly felt proud.

But we also lost something that day. There's a popular post-hoc view that we lost our raison d'être; that Gordon had sought power for its own sake and didn't know what to do once he had it. There's another post-hoc argument that we lost control; that Gordon's previous reliance on set-piece moments and drawn-out decision-making was fundamentally unsuited to the fast-paced and usually random nature of events in No. 10. For me, what we lost that day was something more fundamental, as apparent during the first months of the 'Brown Bounce' as in the doldrums that followed. We lost the Treasury. By which I mean that, in the Treasury, Gordon had officials in every key position who knew how he worked and what he wanted, who knew when to refer issues to him and when to take decisions themselves. These were relationships built up over ten years of long days and late nights working on Budgets, spending reviews, Mansion House speeches and Euro papers. Gordon knew them, and trusted them.

The bulk of the staff Gordon imported into No. 10 were political advisers, with a mish-mash of policy, communications and political responsibilities. By contrast, he took (I believe) just seven civil servants with him from the Treasury, two of those in secretarial roles. He left behind brilliant officials like Mark Bowman – former No. 1 in his private office; Jonathan Black – his speechwriter; Jean-Christophe Gray – No. 2 in his private office; his two most experienced press office aides, Malcolm Graves and Robbie Browse; his events manager, Balshen Izzet; and his parliamentary expert, the aforementioned David Martin. Crucially, he also left behind the dozen or so key Treasury experts who shadowed departmental spending and policy – the 'Home Office guys' and 'Welfare girls' whose advice in each area he relied on. In No. 10, he inherited equally brilliant, equally expert civil servants, but – because there was not the same level of trust and confidence on his side, and the same knowledge of how best to work with him on theirs – the micro-manager within Gordon re-surfaced. When crises like the 2007 foot-and-mouth outbreak or the 2008/9 financial crash demanded micro-management, this was an advantage. But when practised every day, on every issue, it ate into his time, his energy, his mood and his capacity to see the big picture.

I'm not suggesting Gordon could or should have gutted the Treasury of its best officials. Neither Gus O'Donnell nor Nick Macpherson would have allowed it. But if half the time he devoted to trying to recruit junior members of the Blair entourage had been spent negotiating the transfer of even a dozen more of his most trusted Treasury civil servants into key No. 10 roles, he would have been better off. If he'd recorded that YouTube message on expenses in front of Balshen Izzet or Malcolm Graves, they'd have laughed at him and told him to re-record it without the smiles. And if he'd started sounding off in the car with Mark Bowman or Jonathan Black after his encounter with Mrs Duffy, they wouldn't have goaded him by asking, 'What did she say?', they'd have said: 'Forget it. Sign these letters.'

One final thought: Gordon didn't just lose the Treasury on 27 June 2007. The Treasury lost him, with equally far-reaching consequences for the economic crisis in which we now find ourselves… But that's a story for another anniversary.

FIVE YEARS ON: TWENTY-FOUR HOURS OF CRISIS MICRO-MANAGEMENT

2 AUGUST 2012

'RIGHT, THAT BEDROOM window, that side window and that bit of the garden – make sure you're fully clothed at all times,' I said, a bit exhausted and muddy in the doorway of Gordon and Sarah's holiday cottage in Dorset.

I'd just tramped round all the neighbouring fields examining potential vantage points for photographers, and had identified all the points of the property where they could be overlooked. Sarah listened carefully; Gordon muttered darkly about the press being bastards – even though at this point none of them had even worked out where he was, let alone sent snappers to catch him in the nip.

This was Day One of GB's first summer holiday as PM: ahead in the polls, popular with the public and his party, praised by the media, the first twinkling of an autumn election in his eye. My colleagues had volunteered me to spend the first week of my own holiday in the neighbouring village. I was there to deal with any national and local press that started hanging around, to persuade GB that any political story on the news was silly season crap, and most of all to help GB through his No. 10 cold turkey so he'd give us all (including himself) a bloody break.

Besides me there was a rota of Special Branch close protection officers; Peter, a junior civil servant from GB's private office; and two 'Garden Room Girls', so-called because of their office adjoining the Downing Street garden – formidable secretarial staff who can get the President on the phone with one hand, type the Queen's Speech with the other, and fix a fax machine with their feet.

Accompanying the PM on his summer holidays was a prime gig for all No. 10 staff when that meant flying with Tony Blair to Cliff Richard's holiday home in Barbados. Accompanying GB to Dorset did not have quite the same appeal. Nevertheless, within an hour, Peter and the Garden Room Girls had transformed the cottage's conservatory into a fully working prime ministerial office with news tickers, secure phone lines and computers linked to the No. 10 network.

I was keen to get away and start exploring the local pubs, but

GB insisted I stay for dinner and opened a bottle of wine. In a trade full of drinkers and drunks, GB had the greatest dipso-discipline of any politician I ever met. He liked a drink but would only ever touch a drop when he knew there was no more work to do in the day.

We chatted for a while until Peter popped his head round the door. 'Gordon, I've got the office on, they say it's urgent.' GB slammed his wine down. 'Is it a bomb? Get the news on. Why isn't the news on?' He zipped through to the office and I watched him through the glass listening intently then barking instructions. The Garden Room Girls began firing up the electronics; Peter was scribbling down notes. GB gestured me in, hand over the mouthpiece on the phone: 'Foot-and-mouth. Bloody foot-and-mouth.' 'Fuck me,' I said helpfully.

Within minutes, GB was on a conference call with all his top civil servants (most already on holiday), the Chief Vet Debby Reynolds, and Hilary Benn at DEFRA. He told them he'd head back to Downing Street in the morning to chair a COBRA meeting. I swear I could hear the collective groan from London. I should also have been gutted that this was my summer holiday up the Swanee, but all I could think was that I was sitting on a mega-story and most of the papers were nearly in bed.

The mobile signal was flat in the cottage so I ran up the steep road to the motorway, and began my set of phone calls, a media operation that would be impossible to replicate now in the age of Twitter. Nine identical calls to the political editors of the national daily papers:

Hi mate, massive story for you. Just for the editor and the desk in case they want to crash it into the first. But I don't want to see anything on Sky or online. Right? OK. Foot-and-mouth outbreak in Surrey, near Guildford. One farm so far. Symptoms reported yesterday. Test came back positive today. Cows. About fifty. Yeah, five-zero. Testing neighbouring farms to see if it's spread. Gordon's spoken to the Chief Vet, and he's coming back to London in the morning to chair COBRA. Yeah, I know! Massive. Debby Reynolds. Like the actress but with a 'Y'. Spokesman quote: 'We are doing everything in our power to identify the source of this outbreak and control its spread. We are determined to protect the British farming industry.' Right, got to go. Talk later.

Next the BBC, then ITN, then Sky. Then another nine political editors from the Sundays. This was the story that saw the BBC's Gary O'Donoghue being bumped from the ten o'clock news and winning a discrimination compensation payout from the BBC as a result. Good for him, but I've always thought he owes me a pint.

I was up on that motorway hard shoulder for about two hours shouting over the traffic, and when I went back down the road in pitch darkness, I didn't even have enough battery left to light the road in front of me. I got away from the cottage about midnight, had three hours sleep, and was back there at 5 a.m. for the drive back to London. I greeted the protection officers in the driveway. 'Any sign of Gordon?' One of them gestured up at the window, the bedroom window I'd warned GB about, where sure enough, he was peering out into the morning gloom half-naked.

If the previous evening had been a bit chaotic and uncontrolled, GB's mood that morning was still hyperactive but totally clear-thinking. I asked whether he'd slept. 'No, I was reading all this stuff.' He had in his hand the 2002 Iain Anderson report into the government's handling of the 2001 outbreak. One hundred and eighty-seven pages, every one of them read and scribbled on in GB's trademark black felt-tip. In his bag was the Royal Society's report into the science of the 2001 outbreak, also covered in black ink.

The journey back to London was a flurry of phone calls from GB, barking instructions and questions at officials and ministers, all lifted from his study of the Anderson report. Footpaths. Bridle paths. Horse racing. Exports. Tax breaks for farmers and the tourist industry. Cull zones. Exclusion zones. Buffer zones. At times he had a mobile at each ear so that two officials could receive the same orders. I texted a friend saying it was like being with The Wolf from *Pulp Fiction*.

For several hours when we got back to Downing Street, GB stood at the Cabinet table, maps of Surrey spread out in front of him, the brilliant Debby Reynolds describing the likely epidemiology and GB issuing standing instructions on cull zones. Every time he asked how many more livestock would be slaughtered if he stretched the cull zone further, his voice would drop as if the affected cows were listening at the door. I asked him later if it affected him ordering those slaughters, especially when the cattle were probably not infected. He screwed his face up as if to say

'Don't be silly', but then muttered quietly: 'You feel sorry for the little ones.'

In between these meetings, we did a couple of clips and interviews for TV. As with his TV appearances after the June 2007 Haymarket and Glasgow Airport bomb plots, GB won plaudits for the unvarnished, businesslike nature of his statements.

I can't say we deliberately played up to that image, but we certainly didn't try and go the other way. My 'direction' was just: 'Walk up the corridor, speak, take two questions, walk back.' So much simpler than all the 'professionals' over the years who filled GB's head before TV appearances with the 'need' to smile, to face one side or the other, to speak in a certain tone etc.

At the end of those twenty-four hours, even before we were clear how serious the outbreak was, there was no question – whether you were a government official, a political journalist or a punter watching the TV – that the PM was in control of this crisis and was personally directing every aspect of how it would be dealt with.

Of course, people will say that is micro-management gone mad. But sometimes micro-management has its place, and in that moment in 2007 – just like the banking crisis of 2008 – it worked. There are a few thousand farmers and hoteliers who lost their livelihoods in 2001 who probably wish Tony Blair had been a bit more of a micro-manager back then. If there was a fresh outbreak of foot-and-mouth tomorrow in Surrey, I wonder which kind of PM David Cameron would be?

Talking of the current PM, there's an interesting postscript to that twenty-four hours. I recall listening in when GB rang David Cameron to brief him on the latest developments at the Pirbright laboratory, which had by then been identified as the source of the outbreak.

As always, a small group of officials would listen in on these calls, and the tone and content of the call was pretty friendly, with lots of back and forth between them. Towards the end, Cameron asked GB rather plaintively – definitely not joking – when he thought things would stabilise sufficiently so GB would resume his summer holiday and Cameron could resume his. His exact words were: 'I can't go away until you do, and we won't get a holiday at this rate. But you really have to go away first.'

GB laughed and said he'd let him know, but he couldn't go away until the outbreak was contained. The call ended, and GB immediately ran into the outer office and barked at me: 'That was personal, that was private. You don't say a word about that to anyone.'

So not only was the call civilised, which might surprise a few people, but I thought GB's reaction to the holiday remarks indicated his desire to build a decent working relationship for the long-term, not allowing the likes of me to jeopardise it for short-term political advantage.

Later the same day, Cameron did a series of TV interviews very critical of GB's handling of the crisis, using information he'd learnt from their phone call. GB was pretty furious and it made him feel that he couldn't have a relationship with Cameron. It's a familiar criticism of GB that after he'd made up his mind about people, they were either friends for life or he was finished with them (Robin Cook being the notable exception), but at least he gave Cameron a chance.

A GLORY THROUGH THE GLOOM

18 AUGUST 2012

I AM THE GREATEST pessimist who has ever watched a football match. Nothing Arsenal do can ever disappoint me because I go into every match with expectations set at Absolute Zero. Walking to the Emirates, I feel like a follower of William Wallace attending his execution at Smithfield: a sense of duty to be there despite the ordeal I'm expecting.

If we win, I only actually enjoy it for the fleeting moments at the end of injury time when even Arsenal couldn't throw it away, and for five minutes afterwards, before I begin worrying about the next game.

I should say at this point I take no actual pleasure from watching football as a sport, and care nothing for any game not affecting

Arsenal or Celtic. The only times I watched the Euros this summer were to check that our players weren't limping and to wish ill fortune on Scott Parker and Ashley Cole. The latter obliged with his penalty miss for England. Thanks, Ash!

It wasn't always like this. When Paul Davis was playing regularly for Arsenal between 1981 and 1995, and Patrick Vieira between 1996 and 2005, I drew strength and confidence from their peerless brilliance and will to win. And win we did: thirteen trophies split between them over that period; the only players bar Tony Adams to have bridged all that success. Now, as much as I love Koscielny, Sagna and The Ox, none of them give me the same confidence that Davo and Paddy provided.

So a new season begins. And I approach it with the usual pessimism: let's try and snatch fourth; let's finish ahead of Spurs; let's hope the idiots don't start calling for Arsene's head. But some nagging part of me, some distant childhood memory of watching Paul Davis pivot and pirouette and play golf shot passes around Highbury comes back to me, and says: 'Maybe this season will be different'; 'Maybe you'll actually enjoy some games'; 'Maybe Cazorla is as good as they say'. And wherever there's a Maybe, there's Hope.

One of my favourite poems is Thomas Hardy's 'In a Railway Waiting Room' – a desperately depressing vision of Victorian Britain: obsessed by Godless commerce; riven by bloody imperial wars; a fading memory of past rural and maritime glories. And yet, in the joyful expectation of two young children about the day ahead of them, Hardy saw hope, and – however unrealistic – their optimism trumped all the misery in front of him.

I think of that poem at the start of every football season, and –
in anticipation of my drinks at The Eaglet before Saturday's game
against Sunderland – I've adapted Hardy's poem below, for the
first day of the season. So come on you rip-roaring Gunners. Do
it for the kids. Do it for Davo and Paddy. And do it for a pessimistic old git like me.

IN THE EAGLET'S PRE-MATCH DRINK
(WITH PROFUSE APOLOGIES TO THOMAS HARDY)

On a lunchtime sick as a student's sink
With the drizzling gray Of North Holloway,
There were few at the Eaglet's pre-match drink.
About its walls were framed and varnished
Pictures of players, fly-blown, tarnished.
The table bore a sticker-book
For Panini nostalgists to take a look.
I read it for an age,
And, thronging the empty Arsenal page,
Were figures—additions, multiplications
By some one scrawled, with sundry emendations;
Not innocently designed,
But with a greedy mind,
Plainly Van Persie's various offers,
What he could add to his bulging coffers;
And whilst I wondered if there could have been
Any particle of a soul In that wanker at all,

To cypher rates of wage
Upon that printed page,
There joined in the charmless scene
And stood over me and the scribbled book
(To lend the hour's mean hue
A smear of comedy too)
The Bendtner Fan Club, with haggard look
Subdued as stone in their sponsored pants;
And then I heard
From a casual word
They were hoping he'd get just one more chance.
But next there came
For their first home game
In brand-new shirts, children—a pair -
Who laughed at the fly-blown pictures there.
"Here are the Arsenal boys that we,
Mother, are by and by going to see!
When we get there it's 'most sure to be fine,
And the crowd will sing, and the sun will shine!"
It rained on the skylight with a din
As a passing Mackem fan peered in;
But the words of the child in the squalid room
Had spread a glory through the gloom.

Arsenal drew the game with Sunderland 0–0, and endured another season with-
out winning a trophy.

WHAT DAVE CAN LEARN
FROM THE MANXMEN

5 SEPTEMBER 2012

THERE'S A SIMPLE question David Cameron must answer today:

If he believes that a temporary relaxation of planning laws on extensions will stimulate the market, why does he not accept Labour's proposal for a temporary reduction in the VAT rate on home repairs and improvements to help achieve that same effect?

Predictably, he will answer that Labour's solution is always to borrow more and spend more, and we can't have unaffordable tax cuts.

To which the answer is: well, hold on, when the Isle of Man did the same thing, it didn't cost a penny.

Here are the facts:

Under the European Commission's Labour Intensive Services experiment, the Isle of Man cut the VAT rate on home repairs and improvements from 17.5 per cent to 5 per cent from 1 January 2000 to 31 December 2002.

Based on VAT returns and survey data, these were the effects:

- 96 per cent of traders passed on the VAT cut in full;

- 96 per cent said they saw their business increase, with 43 per cent taking on more employees;

- 65 per cent said they saw the shadow economy decrease, with 20 per cent saying customers stopped asking for 'cash-in-hand' deals;

- 40 per cent said customers told them it was work they wouldn't otherwise have had done at all or so soon;

- There was a 14 per cent increase in VAT-registered traders in the relevant sectors;

- Output tax declared by traders carrying out qualifying work (i.e. the amount of VAT they collected from their customers) rose in both 2000 and 2001;

- The output tax collected in qualifying categories rose from £8.5 million in 1999 to £13.25 million in 2001.

So, in summary, there was a massive increase in business, a large proportion of which wouldn't otherwise have taken place, a significant impact on jobs and the shadow economy, and it resulted in more output tax being collected not less.

Obviously a significant element of the success of the scheme was its temporary nature, and it would be more difficult – as the Isle of Man found – to make the case for a permanent reduced rate (other than for the impact on the shadow economy).[6]

My guess is that No. 10 and No. 11 would dearly love to have announced a temporary cut of 15 per cent on VAT on extensions today alongside the relaxation of planning laws, and they could easily have used the Isle of Man evidence to argue that this did not weaken their commitment to deficit reduction.

So why haven't they done it? Because it's part of Labour's Five Point Plan to kick-start the economy (Ed Balls and Ed Miliband were in the Treasury when the Isle of Man experiment took place), and it would look like a concession of defeat to start borrowing policies from the opposition.

But as my good friend, Jason 'Geezer' Brown said on Twitter this morning when I raised this point: 'It's about time all parties

---

6 Incidentally, the reason Gordon was not persuaded to conduct a similar experiment on the mainland was because he felt if he ever cut the VAT rate on anything temporarily, he'd never be able to put it back up (a concern he still had in 2008–9, when the standard rate of VAT was cut for a year to 15 per cent). Plus, in that period, around the time of the Euro assessment and the Kate Barker report, the concern was much more around stimulating new house-building as a way of tackling the housing crisis and stabilising house price inflation, rather than on subsidising homeowners to improve their existing properties. Now the circumstances are pretty different.

stopped playing schoolyard politics and just did what's best for the country!' The Geezer has spoken. Is David Cameron listening?

FOR THE LOVE OF LUTHER

21 SEPTEMBER 2012

THIRTY YEARS AGO today, Luther Vandross issued his second album, *Forever, For Always, For Love*, one of four all-time classic soul/R&B albums he produced, alongside *Never Too Much*, *The Night I Fell in Love* and *Give Me the Reason*. You could make another by taking the best songs from his other albums.[7]

Luther's career – as songwriter, arranger, backing singer and solo artist – spanned four decades. Those who only know him as

---

7 'Superstar/Until You Come Back to Me' from *Busy Body*, 'Any Love' and 'Love Won't Let Me Wait' from *Any Love*, 'Here and Now' from *The Best of Love*, 'Power of Love' and 'I Who Have Nothing' from *Power of Love*, 'Little Miracles' from *Never Let Me Go*, 'Your Secret Love' and 'Goin' Out of my Head' from *Your Secret Love*, and 'Dance with My Father' from *Dance with My Father*.

the voice of saccharine ballads in the latter half of his career are missing a body of work in the 1970s and 1980s which rivals any of the great soul and R&B stars of the last century.

He went from arranging the backing vocals on Bowie's *Young Americans* in 1974 to working with the likes of Bette Midler and Judy Collins, before embracing the disco era, arranging backing vocals for Sister Sledge, Chic and the Streisand/Summer duet 'No More Tears (Enough Is Enough)'. He worked with Chaka Khan at the end of the 1970s alongside a sixteen-year-old Whitney Houston, telling her she would be 'one of the greatest singers that ever lived'.

His breakthrough came in 1980 as one of the lead singers for disco group Change, whose success earned him a solo deal with Epic Records in 1981. The albums that followed in the next six years took him to worldwide fame. They also defied the recording trend of the 1980s towards synthesised beats, his ballads all strings and piano, his upbeat songs all drums and bass guitar, but all the music just a backdrop for his soaring vocals.

His 1981 debut, *Never Too Much*, captured both styles – in the title track (a No. 13 hit in the UK eight years later), and the stand-out track, his incredible reworking of the Burt Bacharach standard, 'A House Is Not a Home', best seen in the astonishing live version in honour of Dionne Warwick at the 1988 NAACP Image Awards.

Throughout his career, from his contribution to *Young Americans* onwards, he had an uncanny ability to hear another artist's work and transform it into something new, epic and distinctively his.[8] Dionne Warwick wept when she first heard his version of 'A House Is Not a Home' because she knew he'd recorded the definitive version, eclipsing her own.

The same was true of his version of The Temptations' 'Since I Lost My Baby' (*Forever, For Always, For Love*), Brenda Russell's 'If Only for One Night' (*The Night I Fell in Love*), Burt Bacharach's 'Anyone Who Had a Heart' (*Give Me the Reason*) and, most astonishingly, on the otherwise fairly average *Busy Body* album (1983), his melding of Stevie Wonder's 'Until You Come Back to Me' and Delaney & Bonnie's 'Superstar', a track so poignant and beautifully sung that it should come with a health warning if you've recently broken up.

I don't think it's a coincidence that all those tracks are about loss and longing, and – along with his much-publicised, depression-fuelled weight fluctuations – the sense of Luther living in a state of sadness and loneliness (captured in the title track of 1998's *Any Love*) was never far away in his songs and interviews.

If it is true – as much rumoured over the years – that he felt he could not be open about his sexuality for fear of alienating his fan base, then it is a thing of great sadness, and we can only be glad Frank Ocean – a worthy heir to Luther if ever there was one – has not done the same.

My own love affair with Luther started in 1986 in my second year at Christchurch Secondary School in Friern Barnet, when I met

---

8 Although, strangely enough, one of his most disappointing albums – 1994's *Songs* – was a whole collection of cover versions, one of which – his 'Endless Love' duet with Mariah Carey – became the biggest hit of his career.

a girl named Virna Milsom. A mutual love of Alexander O'Neal's 'If You Were Here Tonight' led to her lending me Luther's first four albums, including *Forever, For Always, For Love*. When his fifth album – *Give Me the Reason* – got to No. 3 in the UK charts in September that year, I was in a position to say knowingly that I preferred the older, less commercial stuff!

I left Christchurch aged fourteen to attend Finchley Catholic High School and, in the last throes of unrequited love for Virna, I bought her a bottle of Ysatis perfume and said I'd got us two tickets to see Luther at Wembley Arena. She accepted the perfume but declined the ticket. I took my mum instead but, next year, I was there on my own twice during his then record-breaking ten-night run at the Arena, every night a sell-out.

Over the years, I was there again on my own every time he played Wembley Arena (he is second only to Cliff Richard in all-time appearances). The one exception was his 'Your Secret Love' tour in November 1997. As always, I had one ticket, but I'd started going out with my dream girl from university ten days beforehand and when she told me she was feeling blue, I skipped the concert and took her out for dinner instead. There'll always be another time, I thought, and Luther would approve of my reasons.

There wasn't another time. He never toured the UK again. In 2003, he recorded his last album *Dance with My Father*, the title track from which would go on to win the Best Song Grammy for 2004. Shortly afterwards, he had a severe stroke and never sang again. He died on 1 July 2005, at the age of just fifty-four.

So today, I'll have *Forever, For Always, For Love* on repeat:

tapping my feet to the happy, upbeat songs like 'She Loves Me Back'; shivering at the spare soulfulness of the brilliant 'Promise Me'. And I'll raise a glass to the greatest soul singer of the 1980s, and one of the great loves of my life.

THE TRAGIC TALE OF JOHN BARRON

26 SEPTEMBER 2012

WHEN I WAS researching the lives and deaths of Finchley Catholic Grammar School students who died in the Second World War and its aftermath, one of the most tragic I came across was that of John Barron, who died on this day seventy years ago. That was even before I discovered a sad twist to his story, courtesy of his nephew Robert.

John was born in 1929 into a large family which split its time between Folkestone in Kent and a cottage in the Pas-de-Calais in France. He attended Finchley Catholic School from 1933–36, the third of four brothers to do so, and joined the Merchant Navy when war broke out.

His family were still living in France when the Wehrmacht invaded, and – as British nationals in a prime location on the Channel coast – the Nazis decided they were a spying risk. They were arrested and interned at a camp in Troyes, eastern France, where John's father Ernest died, although from natural causes, not as a result of Nazi brutality as the school magazine reported at the time.

John became a signalman in the Merchant fleet, and he had already survived one torpedo attack in the Mediterranean when he was posted to the convoys taking essential supplies across the North Atlantic, running the gauntlet of the U-boat 'Wolfpacks' patrolling the freezing seas.

In September 1942, he joined the crew of the SS *Boston* – an American pleasure-steamer loaned to the Allied convoys, journeying from Newfoundland to the UK. One fellow crew member, a 33-year-old named Billy Wells from Liverpool, wrote to his family that he was 'sailing home in an orange box with an engine, not sea-worthy for a park lake, let alone the Atlantic Ocean'.

On 21 September, the *Boston* set sail with a cargo of ballast alongside seven other ships carrying low-value cargo in Convoy RB1. On the 24th, Captain Young of the *Boston* ordered signals to be sent by lamp to his counterparts on the other ships. As signalman, it is possible that John himself sent the chilling message. It read: 'We Are Being Followed. Expect Attack Tonight.'

The attack came the following morning from the Blitz Wolfpack: seventeen submarines deployed to attack what their intelligence had told them was a troopship convoy carrying 25,000 men. Three torpedoes from U-216 hit the *Boston*, and it quickly capsized by the stern. However, all sixty-five crew members – including John – were evacuated onto lifeboats and picked up by the British Destroyer, HMS *Veteran*.

Sadly, the attack was not over, and the Wolfpack continued its pursuit of the Convoy, now badly in disarray with three of eight ships sunk. U-404, one of the deadliest submarines in the German fleet, captained by the highly decorated Otto von Bulow, tracked down HMS *Veteran* on the morning of 26 September, and sank her with two direct hits.[9]

Almost 300 crewmen went into the water from HMS *Veteran*, and only two survived. Remarkably, both had also survived the sinking of the *Boston*, and eventually made it back to Britain aboard their rescue ship, SS *New Bedford*. But John was not one of them, and he perished in the north Atlantic at the age of twenty-three.

Since the war, there has been controversy over the fate of convoys like RB1. The families of victims have asked why they were carrying low-value cargo in unsuitable ships in such dangerous waters, and whether they were actually decoys for the vital movements of troopships elsewhere across the Atlantic. They wonder why the Wolfpack which attacked RB1 had false intelligence that it was a troopship convoy.

---

9 As for the U-Boats which attacked Convoy RB1, U-216 was sunk off the Irish coast a few weeks later with the loss of all its crew, the *Boston* being the only ship it sank. The U-404 survived a few more months but was sunk with the loss of all its crew in the Bay of Biscay in June 1943. By then, its commander – Otto von Bulow – had been promoted to a shore position. He survived the war, dying in 2006 at the age of ninety-four.

We may never know the full truth or appreciate the agonising decisions that those in command had to make, and the uncertainty will not have made it any easier for the families and friends of victims like John Barron to bear their loss. But he died doing his duty, and did so incredibly bravely, and that must be remembered above all.

John's name stands on the Chatham Naval Memorial in Kent, not far from his childhood home, alongside more than 10,000 other sailors from World War Two whose bodies were lost to the sea.

The *Albanian* school magazine for 1943 recorded his death as follows:

> John was the second of three brothers [*sic*] who succeeded each other as conspicuous members of Feckenham House. Early this year, we learnt from his eldest brother that John – missing since last September – is now considered definitely lost at sea.
>
> We gather from friends at Halifax that he was anxious to be in England for Christmas and asked for a ship; he left the very next day. To his widowed mother and bereaved home we send our tenderest sympathy.

Shortly after his death, in a painful postscript, John's family received personal effects he had left in Canada, including a diary, a grocery receipt for tea, marmalade and sugar (luxuries amidst wartime rationing in Britain), as well as letters posted to John from an address in South Africa via his late father's solicitors in London.

In the weeks following his death, further letters written by

John from Canada to be forwarded to South Africa also arrived at the solicitors. From the content of these letters, John's family discovered that he had been involved in a secret relationship with a male army officer, using the solicitors' office as a conduit for their correspondence.

It should be remembered that during the war, and for many years afterwards, a serviceman caught in a same-sex relationship could in theory be court-martialled and jailed, or at least given hard labour as a punishment.

The South African army officer therefore addressed his letters to 'Jean Barron', and John signed his letters the same way. Both men avoided writing anything incriminating in their letters, simply stating their longing to see each other again.

Anyone intercepting their letters en route would have believed it was correspondence between a man and a woman, and no one at John's base would have batted an eyelid at him receiving correspondence from his father's solicitor using the French form of 'John'.

John's family have taken comfort over the years that he had known some secret happiness away from the war before dying so young, although they also faced the sadness of leaving unanswered several letters from South Africa received by the solicitor after John had gone missing, as the army officer anxiously sought news of his whereabouts.

We do not know what became of him, but let us hope he survived the war and lived to find happiness afterwards. And let us hope that John Barron continues to rest in peace.

THE HEROISM OF
SGT FRANK MITCHELL

27 SEPTEMBER 2012

FRANK MITCHELL WAS one of three brothers from Barnet who attended Finchley Catholic Grammar School in its earliest years. He joined the small classroom in the Dale Grove presbytery in 1927, and remained at FCGS for seven years. A year in the seminary at St Edmund's followed, where he gained his school certificate and played rugby for the First XI, but he decided not to pursue a career in the priesthood and instead joined the RAF shortly after the outbreak of war.

On the morning of 7 September 1941, Frank took off on a training flight out of RAF Abingdon in an Avro Anson N9617. There were two wireless operators, Frank and Sgt Raymond Keen, and two navigators, Sgt Leslie Copland and P/O J. E. Taylor. The pilot was Thomas Weller, a native of Hendon, with more than 1,000 hours' flying experience.

As the plane neared the Berwyn Hills in Wales, it entered dense cloud and mist. Copland warned the pilot he was too low, and Weller began a steep climb. It was too late. The plane crashed head-on into the sloping side of the Moel Sych, a 2,713 ft mountain, the highest peak in the Berwyns and the scourge of many other aircraft before and since.

The Anson's wings were ripped off as it crashed up the mountainside. P/O Weller was thrown against his flying column and killed. The plane came to a rest: a mess of twisted wreckage, leaking fuel and the injured bodies of the four surviving airmen. Sgt Copland was trapped by collapsed metal rods, with a broken thigh bone and a huge open wound on his broken forearm. He could not free himself from the wreckage.

Taylor was bleeding badly from a gashed head, Keen had cuts all over his body, and Frank Mitchell – who had been thrown against his wireless equipment – had bad injuries to his face, knees and legs. All three were able to crawl out of the wreckage onto the misty mountainside. If rescue did not come before nightfall, they and Copland were bound to die from either blood loss or exposure. It was Frank who volunteered to go for help.

Edward Doylerush, author of *Fallen Eagles*, takes up the story:

> Keen gave first aid as best as he could to his two comrades.
> Together they watched as Mitchell was swallowed up in the

all-enveloping mist. Due to the nature of his injuries, he was often forced to crawl down the mountainside on his hands and knees, and progress was painfully slow. The terrain was terrible, being covered in an unending succession of clumps of heather, bilberry, and cottongrass – all competing for space and to stop him.

The lie of the land pushed him to the right and he eventually came to a stream in a ravine where he drank the refreshing clear water. Later, the stream entered the Alon Disgynfa and the course of this small river was followed.

A long time later the river vanished over the high waterfall of Pistyll Rhaeadr with high ground beyond the river and a steep escarpment to the left. He had come out of the mist and could see no alternative to save time than to slide over the escarpment, and let himself down hanging onto clumps of grass and the roots of trees exposed on the rocks.

With a drop of over 200 feet in places, Mitchell was fortunate not to break his neck, which would also have had serious consequences for the other crew members still on the mountain. As he reached the boulder strewn area at the foot of the cliffs, he saw a narrow valley with a country lane leading away. Not only that, but nestled in the trees at the foot of the falls was a cottage.

His descent had taken three hours, and now he was faced with climbing a stone wall which faced him. He could not use his legs to climb over, so pulled himself up with his arms and rolled over, falling heavily on the other side. The sudden movement was caught at the window of the cottage by Mrs Woodcock, an

> evacuee from Liverpool, who had taken the cottage for a while.
> She was very thin and known locally as 'The Human Hairpin',
> but she had the strength to help Mitchell into the cottage.

Mrs Woodcock summoned help, and Frank was able to tell the rescue party the location of the crashed plane. Help soon reached Frank's crewmates, Copland was cut from the wreckage, and all four were taken to the hospital at Gobowen in Shropshire where they were treated for their injuries by Dr Reginald Watson Jones, who went on to become a pioneering surgeon and King George VI's personal orthopaedic doctor.[10]

In January 1942, the *London Gazette* reported that Frank Mitchell would be awarded the British Empire Medal, the decoration below the George Cross for acts of meritorious service and gallantry. The citation said: 'As a result of this airman's devotion to duty, the rescue of other members of the crew was made possible by nightfall. There is no doubt that, but for his action, they would have succumbed to their injuries.'

A month later, Frank visited FCGS with his brother Tony. They spoke at an assembly of the senior school held in the entrance hall of the White House, and Father Parsons led the congratulations

---

10 As for the men whose lives Frank saved thanks to his arduous scramble down the Moel Sych, we do not know what became of P/O Taylor, but we know that Leslie Copland and Raymond Keen both recovered from their injuries to fly again and both survived the war in PoW camps after being shot down in bombing raids over Germany. Raymond Keen was imprisoned in the notorious Stalag Luft III camp in April 1943. A year later, the camp was witness to 'The Great Escape', when seventy-seven officers tunnelled out from the north compound, fifty of them later murdered by the Nazis in cold blood after their capture, three making successful escapes to neutral countries.

to Frank on becoming the first Old Boy to be awarded military honours.

Having recovered from his injuries, Frank rejoined the 10th Operational Training Unit at Abingdon. On 27 September 1942, he was acting as Wireless Operator in a Whitley BD576 at Stanton Harcourt airfield. The pilot was practising overshoot procedures when he climbed too steeply away from the landing strip. The plane stalled and crashed to the ground.

This time there was no escape, and Frank was killed instantly along with the rest of the crew. It was just two days before he was due to be presented with his British Empire Medal by King George VI. He was aged twenty-six, and left a young widow.

A packed congregation gathered at Barnet for his Requiem Mass on 2 October, with staff and pupils of the school singing in the choir and the entire FCGS Sixth Form present. Frank was buried in the Bells Hill burial ground in Barnet. *The Albanian* records that: 'The impressive ceremony was a fitting close to the life of a hero of whom his family, his School and his Parish are rightly proud.'

THE SEVEN-YEAR HITCH

1 OCTOBER 2012

EIGHT YEARS AGO today in Washington DC, I endured – no other way to describe it – one of the toughest days in my working life. And it had all started so well.

Still a civil servant at that stage, I watched the 2004 Labour Party conference in Brighton from my office in the Treasury. Compared to the acrimony of the 2003 conference ('Best when we are Labour' etc.), Brighton had been relatively harmonious, and all the speculation was that a deal had secretly been done for TB to stand down for GB before the 2005 election or shortly afterwards.

GB met us at Heathrow ebullient and firing on all cylinders.

He'd made huge play in his conference speech of our obligations to the poorest in the world, and was now hyperactive about the need to deliver progress at the G7 summit in Washington. This suited me. He'd spend the flight talking to Shriti Vadera, Jon Cunliffe and his other international development experts about negotiating strategy. I could spend it drinking my way through BA's wine list and watching films.

Scattered throughout the plane were the various economics editors of the national broadsheets – Larry Elliott from *The Guardian*, Gary Duncan from *The Times*, Phil Thornton from *The Indie* – and up in business class with us were the legendary Alex Brummer from the *Daily Mail* and the greatest journalist you've never heard of, Sumeet Desai, then of Reuters.

We landed in bright sunshine at Dulles and, as usual, I had my two phones out and switched on as we were descending, ready to pick up the latest from London. Not that I was especially obsessed, but I could guarantee Gordon's first question as we walked off the plane would be: 'What's the news?' If we'd ever been taken hostage by the Taliban in Kabul, rescued by the SAS, and dragged into a helicopter, Gordon's first question to me when they took the hoods off would have been: 'What's the news?'

I looked at my phones. My inbox was starting to fill up like a Tetris board – thirty-six messages, eighteen voicemail notifications. I went through the texts. Ed Balls: 'Ring as soon as you land.' Ian Austin: 'Ring ASAP.' Trevor Kavanagh: 'Are you in Washington with GB? A word when you can.' Phil Webster: 'Give us a call.' Ian Austin: 'If there are press on that plane, get them well away from GB.' Steve Field: 'Blimey. Carnage.' Ed Balls: 'Ensure total discipline.' Ian Austin: 'Have you not landed yet?'

It's at these moments that three thoughts go through your head: 1. Oh shit; 2. Why does no one take the time to send you a text which helpfully and succinctly explains what the hell is going on?; and 3. Oh shit.

As we were taxiing down the runway, I called Ian then Ed. Ian: 'No. 10 had to announce that Blair's having a heart operation tomorrow and explain why he's bought a house in Connaught Square, so he's tried to get on top of it by saying he'll serve a full third term. It's all being done as a devastating blow to Brown – kills his chances of becoming PM and so on. Total carnage.' Ed: 'You've got one job – Gordon and everyone around him needs to be totally disciplined about this. Total discipline.'

The door opened and the business class passengers went down the steps into a shuttle bus. I'd had to break terrible news to GB over the years – that was part of my job. When we worked in No. 10, I became the official 'breaker of bad news' because I was regarded as the best at it. But aside from the death of Robin Cook, this was the hardest thing I ever had to tell him.

Gordon: 'What's in the news?' Me: 'Hold on.' Gordon: 'What's wrong? What's happening?' Me: 'I need you to tell you something, but you can't react. You're being watched by Alex Brummer.' Gordon (agitated): 'What is it?' Me: 'You need to relax. Alex is watching to see if you're angry or upset, so you need to calm down before I tell you.'

When I relayed the news, his head started to sink, but he then put on his famous fixed grin for Alex's benefit and started talking about where we would watch the weekend's football matches. When we got to the convoy of cars and minibuses to take us to the IMF building, GB disappeared into his limousine and I got on with the job of 'ensuring total discipline', telling all the officials and advisers with us that both we and Gordon would be under massive media scrutiny for the next twenty-four hours for evidence of anger or depression, so it was vital that no one gave them any.

It was already too late. As we later discovered, somewhere, somehow, between the plane landing and GB's entourage going into the IMF, the brilliant Larry Elliott – not just the best economic journalist in the world but one of the most intrepid newshounds in the British media – had managed to get a corker of a quote out of one of our number: 'It's like an African coup – they waited 'til he was out of the country.'

Once inside the UK delegation office at the IMF – then occupied by Tom Scholar, currently occupied by Alex Gibbs (the greatest Treasury civil servant of the last twenty years), and soon to be occupied by David Cameron's official spokesman Steve Field – the mood was pitch black. GB had a series of scheduled meetings with other delegations, but could barely be prised away from Tom's sofa, where he sat staring out of the window at the street below.

I stood nearby, making my series of calls to the umpteen political journalists who had texted me asking for the reaction from Washington and for details of Gordon's mood and movements, sounding as bright and relaxed as I could, explaining that he was busy with his meetings, had no problem with Tony's statement and was fixated on getting increased IMF aid for developing countries, GB occasionally looking darkly at me as if he thought I was chiding him.

That evening, as usual when we were overseas, the Media Monitoring Unit at No. 10 faxed me through the front pages of the papers, asking with more than their usual sarcasm: 'Are you interested in the coverage of the PM's statement?' As the *Guardian* splash rolled off the fax machine with its 'African coup' headline, my heart sunk and my head raged. Others at home were seeing it at the same time, and my phone started to hum again. Ian: 'Have you seen *Guardian*? Who the hell said that?' Ed: 'What happened to discipline?!' Trevor Kavanagh: 'Just seen *Guardian*. An urgent word please.'

The Treasury under GB was almost immune to unplanned leaks and rogue quotes, a remarkable record sustained over ten years. That was in part due to our policy that unless a quote came from X, Y or Z, then we'd simply deny that it represented the Treasury view, where X was the Head of Communications (successively Peter Curwen, John Kingman, Michael Ellam, me, Paul Kissack and Chris Martin), Y was the Media Special Adviser (successively Charlie Whelan, Ian Austin and me), and Z was Gordon himself or either of the two Eds.

It was also due – and I take full credit/responsibility for this – to my Admiral Byng approach to leaks. If anything did appear in the papers that was not from X, Y or Z, I would instantly name a culprit. I'd try to choose someone who was a decent suspect, but their guilt didn't really matter – it was the assertion of their guilt that mattered. They would be cut out of meetings, removed from the circulation list for emails, and wherever they walked in the Treasury, people would mutter about their demise. The effect of this was to make the actual guilty party feel guilty as hell, and put the fear of God into everyone else in the Treasury about doing any leaking themselves. As for the poor Admiral Byngs, they'd usually recover after a while, and some of them were probably guilty anyway.

With the 'African coup' quote, the chief suspect was Shriti, although she furiously and plausibly denied responsibility, and she was too important to GB to give her the Admiral Byng treatment. So I had to let it slide and, to this day, Larry remains inscrutable on the subject.

That evening, I sat with GB at the hotel bar, and watched the first presidential debate between John Kerry and George W. Bush. In six years working for GB, I never saw him so down. Within ten minutes of the debate starting, he was rasping criticism at his friend John Kerry. 'Look what Bush is doing – security, security, security. He's defining the election, and instead of challenging him, Kerry's going along with it. He's trying to win on security – he'll never win on security. Where's the economy? Where's jobs? Madness. Madness. He's just lost the election.'

As each question was asked by the debate moderator, Gordon would thump the bar and deliver a word-perfect response for Kerry to deliver, and then thump the bar again and shake his head as Kerry made his own response. 'Rubbish. Total rubbish. You've lost, man. You've lost.' It was a remarkable thing to watch,

GB gripped by anger and frustration, projecting his own feelings onto Kerry, but still the consummate political genius.

Later that night, I tried to cheer GB up. 'Look, Blair was forced into making that statement – he didn't want to make it, and he probably doesn't believe it – he had to say it or else he'd have to quit before the election. Nothing's really changed – he's not going to serve another five years.' GB just shook his head.

'I've already had seven years. Once you've had seven years, the public start getting sick of you. You've got seven years when you've got a chance to get people on board, but after that, you're on the down slope. I've tried not to be too exposed, but it's still seven years. The only chance was getting in next year before the election. Tony knows that. Every year that goes by, the public are going to say: "Not that guy Brown, we're tired of him – give us someone new."'

We talked a while about the 'seven years' theory. It was clearly informed by the US presidential system, but GB went through a series of British politicians and made the same point. He argued that Margaret Thatcher – despite carefully rationing her public appearances (a point made by Peter Bingle in his Friday musing) – was on the slide in public opinion even at the time of the 1987 election, and that Churchill had only bucked the trend by continually reinventing himself.

I understood GB's mood and mindset far better after that conversation. I believe he only ever wanted to fight and win one election, serve four years and hand over to the next generation before the following election. He believed 2005 was his one chance to do that, and Tony's statement had robbed him of that chance.

Of course, he robbed himself of his second chance in 2007, but that's another story.

There was an amusing postscript to that dark day. The next morning, GB had to do his briefing to the UK economics editors in a meeting room in the IMF building. As he prepared to go in, he asked what he should say if anyone asked him about Tony's heart operation. Sue Nye said that Anji Hunter was due to text her when they knew that the operation had been a success and Tony was recovering, but she'd heard nothing yet. GB was only half-listening, and when he sat down with the journalists, he began his briefing by saying: 'I'm sure you'll all be glad to hear that Tony Blair's heart operation has been successful and he's recovering well, and we all wish him well.'

Sumeet Desai was hovering at the back of the room, and raised his eyebrows at me in time-honoured 'Can I go and use that?' fashion. Having only half-heard what Sue said myself, I gave him a nod. He slipped out and five minutes later – as Adam Boulton, Nick Robinson and the world's press stood outside No. 10 saying that there was no news yet from No. 10 or the hospital on the PM's condition – the 'breaking news' flashed up: 'Reuters: Brown says Blair operation "successful"; PM "recovering well"' – much to the chagrin of the journalists in Downing Street and the confusion of Tony's staff given he was still under sedation at the time.

Why does any of this matter today? Well, next Wednesday marks seven years since David Cameron's 'speech without notes' at the 2005 Tory conference, so we will soon get a chance to test the theory again. Cameron obviously hasn't been PM for all of that time, but he was the most over-exposed opposition leader in history, and has undoubtedly been front line in the public consciousness for seven years. Indeed, three of the top 'Family Fortunes' associations the public has with Cameron (i.e. 'What comes into your head when you think about David Cameron?') – huskies, hoodies and chauffeurs – will also see their 7th anniversaries within the next ten months.

But as Peter Bingle again observed in that Friday musing, the interesting thing is that Tory strategists are currently trying to recreate the ubiquity that the PM enjoyed in his first year as opposition leader: putting him on *Letterman*, putting him in every Olympic arena, even – heaven help us – putting him on Twitter.

If Gordon's seven-year theory is right, this is the last thing they should be doing; they should be rationing his public appearances and building up other fresher individuals – especially the exceptional Grant Shapps – as the public face of the Tory Party. Otherwise, they risk people switching on the pre-election debates in 2015, looking at Cameron and thinking: 'Oh, not you again. I can't stand another five years of you.'

That's if Gordon's theory is right. We'll wait and see. But in the meantime, anyone who complains that Ed Miliband isn't ubiquitous enough should remember that he was in Washington with GB that weekend, he heard the same mantra, and he knows that by the time of the next election, he will already have been four-and-a-half years in the job. So excuse him if he plays the long game when building his public profile. He's smart is Ed Miliband.

THE SEVEN BASIC
PLOTS OF POLITICS

2 OCTOBER 2012

THERE ARE SEVEN basic plots in politics.

Just as in Christopher Booker's analysis of literature and film, I believe there are seven basic stories being played out in the careers of almost all significant politicians, which repeat themselves endlessly, and have done for centuries:

1. Principled or maverick individual succeeds because of their principled or maverick approach; power changes them, leaving their supporters disappointed.

2. Charismatic would-be king is thwarted by ruthless, unworthy opponents; ends up exiled and frustrated in life.

3. For years, the heir to the throne yearns restlessly for the crown; finally gets it – at some price – but fortune turns against them.

4. Two individuals rise to power together, but eventually destroy one another, either through blind loyalty or the emergence of distrust.

5. A great individual has one fatal flaw or makes one great mistake which undoes them and damages their reputation.

6. A ruthless leader lives and dies by the sword, destroyed by their own pride and paranoia, and often assassinated by their own protégés.

7. A canny foot-soldier rises to the top, using the mind more than the sword, but is never comfortable with power and is replaced by a more natural born leader.

There are three other plots which exist purely in political fiction:

1. The thwarted and exiled would-be king comes back a wiser, stronger person, takes the crown, and rules successfully.

2. A young rogue with bad habits or fatal flaws corrects their

habits and flaws, becomes a changed person, and rules successfully.

3. The principled or maverick individual retains their principled or maverick approach even when they obtain power, and rules successfully.

Of course, all these plots – other than the fictional ones – end in failure, and those politicians who manage to navigate a successful end to their careers are so rare that they don't warrant a 'plot' of their own.

But it's a useful exercise for politicians to look at that list of standard plots, work out which film they're in and what fate they're headed for, and try to change the script. For that reason, I believe every politician should be a film and literature buff – able to recognise a narrative arc when they see one, and have a clear sense of how the story will play out.

That brings me to the film that David Cameron and his entourage watched on the eve of the Conservative Party conference a year ago today.

*   *   *

HAMBURGER HILL

Whether it was the watching of the film that inspired the naming of the strategy, or the naming of the strategy that inspired the watching of the film, we know – from Allegra Stratton's fine column written a couple of weeks later – that senior Tories now refer to their economic and deficit strategy as 'Hamburger Hill'.

For those who have not seen the film, it's a realistic if formulaic depiction of one squad's experience during the American assault on Hill 937 near the Laos border in May 1969, and it's easy to see why it inspired David Cameron.

From his point of view, the parallels are obvious. The hill is a hugely challenging target with an entrenched enemy, against which the Americans launch a relentless, full-frontal assault. In the film, the squad – despite heavy casualties – retain their morale and camaraderie, and stick to their mission; they rail against the lily-livered critics back home and the media doubting their ability to get the job done; and at the end of the film, exhausted but triumphant, they bask in their hard-won victory.

The trouble is if the Tories look beyond the fictionalised account, they'd have learnt that the real Hill 937 battle is viewed as a tactically inept, strategically pointless disaster, encapsulated in the fact that – unmentioned in the film – the Americans surrendered the hill just days after finally capturing it. The unacceptably high casualties from the battle succeeded in turning American public opinion even more firmly against the war, and led the White House to order an end to similar operations. Not exactly the model for economic policy, it seems.

Of course, there is an interesting parallel between Vietnam and the current debate about the government's economic and deficit strategy.

Just as in Vietnam, many individuals within government and the media are telling themselves that if the Osborne strategy doesn't seem to be working in terms of delivering economic growth or bringing the deficit down, it's not that the strategy is the wrong one, it's just not being implemented fast enough or on a big enough scale. Thus in Vietnam, successive American administrations carried themselves deeper and deeper into the quagmire, at unimaginable cost to their own forces, to American society, and – most of all – to the people of Vietnam, Laos and Cambodia.

If David Cameron is indeed taken by Vietnam films, he could do worse on the eve of his conference next weekend than watch *The Fog of War*, the brilliant series of interviews with former US Defense Secretary Robert Macnamara charting the descent into the Vietnam quagmire and hearing his regrets about all the missed opportunities to change course. Unlike *Hamburger Hill*, that film has the virtue of being the truth.

Incidentally, watching Ed Balls's speech earlier, I was reminded by his 'Butch Cameron' line of an important movie parallel in terms of Labour's economic strategy.

Two years ago, almost every senior voice in the Labour Party – with the exception of the trade union bosses – was telling the party they had two choices: they could either back the Tory economic and deficit strategy 100 per cent in an attempt to neutralise the issue; or they could back the speed of the proposed deficit reduction plan, but disagree with some of the specifics about where the cuts and tax rises should fall.

With either option, Labour would have been damned in 2015. If they backed the pace of deficit reduction and the Osborne plan succeeded, then the coalition would be able to claim they'd achieved their mission and deserved another term in office, regardless of any disputes about how the deficit had been reduced. But if Labour backed the plan and it failed, the public would tar all parties with the blame, again regardless of any nuances over where the cuts had fallen.

Ed Balls introduced the third choice: opposing the pace of deficit reduction and saying the whole strategy would prove counterproductive. If he was wrong, Labour were damned anyway. If he was right, then they'd have the chance of a hearing with the public. He did the only thing that gave Labour a chance.

It reminded me of the scene in *Butch Cassidy and the Sundance Kid* where the posse has the pair trapped on the edge of a ravine. Their only choices are to 'give' and go to prison, or 'fight', in which case they'd be killed or starved out.

Butch Cassidy introduces the third choice – jumping off the ravine – the most dangerous of all the options but the only one that gives them a chance.

Obviously there was a bit more economic theory at work when Balls defined Labour's position on the deficit, but I'd like to think there was a bit of the film buff at work as well. Either way, as long as he and Ed Miliband avoid both Bolivia and Plot 4 in my list, they might just succeed.

FIVE YEARS ON:
THE ELECTION THAT NEVER WAS

6 OCTOBER 2012

PREFACE

Ever since I started writing this blog, I've had the date 6 October in my mind – five years on from the election that never was, undoubtedly the worst day of my working life, and a disastrous day for the Labour Party and for Gordon Brown in particular. It's not the pain of remembering that day that's been on my mind, but how to write about it without simply giving 'my side' of a story that's already been told more ways than *Rashomon*, and without telling people things they already know from reading the various contemporary newspaper accounts and subsequent biographies.[11]

Most of all, I've wanted to avoid – in a way that others frankly haven't – talking about this issue just in order to settle scores or stir bad blood. For example, I used to dream of confronting Spencer Livermore over the bare-faced lies he told Steve Richards about events on 6 October 2007, but the benefit of a few years' perspective has taken the heat out of those feelings, and made me feel: 'What's the point?' So what I've tried to do below – rather than a blow-by-blow account – is simply give some personal reflections on ten key moments and memories from the run-up to that day, the day itself, and the aftermath. Apologies in advance for the length of this piece.

THE WISDOM OF WHITE

Many people have argued that at the first hint of newspaper speculation – fuelled by the ever-increasing poll leads of July, August

---

11 6 October previously marked my favourite political anniversary – the day that betting duty was abolished in 2001 and replaced with a gross profits tax on bookmakers – a reform which saved the British high-street bookmaking industry and stopped betting in this country disappearing exclusively online and offshore. I was the lead official in the Treasury's tax policy team, although the credit for driving through the reforms sits with my then boss, Alex Gibbs. We managed to bring forward implementation by three months from January, and I drafted a press notice which – to save the tabloids a job – included the top ten bets that punters would be able to have tax-free between October and Christmas as a result of the earlier start date: Sol Campbell to score for Arsenal on his return to Spurs; Robbie Williams to get the Christmas No. 1 etc. The Treasury press office loved it and it was all set to go, but when GB was asked to sign off his quote, the old Presbyterian in him was furious: 'What are you doing encouraging gambling? This is the Treasury, not bloody Las Vegas!' The original press notice was scrapped and something that was potentially a very popular announcement with punters was reduced to a bland technical note. GB's moral compass at work!

and September – we should have announced that there would under no circumstances be an early election. The truth is that Gordon's pollsters were telling him this was a unique opportunity: his personal ratings and the Labour poll lead were beyond anything they'd expected, and the strong feeling was that they would never be this good again.

If you'll forgive the football metaphor, it's like an away team finding themselves 3–0 up after ten minutes at Old Trafford. Sit back and defend, and you allow United back into the game. The best option is to keep attacking, get the crowd on United's back, keep their defence in disarray, and see if you can get another couple of goals. So once the speculation started, the instinct wasn't to rule out an election, but to keep attacking.

And much as the media later blamed GB and his team for all that, they too were players rather than observers. It suited them because it was an exciting story, but more than that, every journalist had a personal view on whether we should or shouldn't 'go for it'. Some on the right thought Cameron was an empty suit and wanted an early election to get rid of him. Some on the left thought we needed longer to win back voters who'd left over Iraq. Some just had skiing holidays booked, and would get their diaries out and say, 'I don't mind what you do, but not before November.'

There was only one journalist I spoke to through that entire period – *The Guardian*'s Michael White – whose view was simply: 'You will regret this speculation. Either way you go, the speculation is bad for you, and you've got to stop it. Announce what you're doing now and stick to it.' He talked about how Jim Callaghan had misjudged things in 1978, and how we risked doing the same. He was spot-on.

'BUILD UP THE YOUNG GUYS'

Following Gordon's speech at the start of the Labour conference, we watched the early-evening news in his hotel suite in Bournemouth. The previous year in Manchester, I had watched the post-speech smile fall from his face as I told him about Cherie Blair's 'That's a lie' outburst, but a year later, he was beaming. However, I told him we were going to have a problem filling up the rest of the week with anything other than election frenzy – with every news outlet wanting to be the first to make it official, and reading huge amounts into every word emerging from those in the know.

He narrowed his eyes: 'Build up the Young Guys. Turn it into a beauty contest about who'll take over from me. Don't for God's sake say I won't serve a full term, but say "Brown doesn't want to go on forever. Brown will start putting the next generation into all the senior posts, and one of them will become leader." Then Cameron can't use youth against me. We'll say: "They've got one young guy in charge, and that guy Osborne, but Labour's got all the best young talent coming through."'

I asked him who he wanted me to talk up as potential future leaders when I briefed this out to the media. His eyes narrowed again, and he reeled off surnames like a football manager naming his First XI: 'Purnell. Miliband. Kelly. Burnham. Cooper. Balls. Miliband.' I replied: 'You've already said Miliband' GB: 'Both of them.' Me: 'Really? You want me to say Ed Miliband?' He looked surprised: 'You need to watch Ed Miliband, he's the one to watch.'

With my Treasury background, I'd found it hard enough to get used to the two Eds being MPs, let alone one of them leading the party. He carried on: 'You know you'll have to choose between them one day. Who will you back?' 'I'm closer to Ed Miliband,' I said. 'Don't base it on who you're close to,' he said, 'base it on who you believe in.' That relaxed, confident conversation convinced me, first, that we were definitely going for the early election; and second, that GB was already planning to hand over to 'the next generation' for a post-Olympics election in 2012.

Two hours later, I was back in GB's suite with the mood totally transformed by *The Times*'s splash accusing him of plagiarising speeches by John Kerry and others, an occupational hazard when you had the great US consultant Bob Shrum writing for both men. He was fuming over the suggestion that he'd ripped off his 'moral compass' language from John Kerry, mainly because he'd first used it in his father's funeral eulogy. There was no calming him, and he wasted twenty-four hours defending his integrity rather than thinking about handling the election announcement, a pattern that would repeat itself in 2009 when the *Telegraph* broke the expenses scandal with a story about his cleaning bills.

NOT ONE SOLITARY SEAT

Following the Labour conference, the Tories began briefing that even to cut Labour's majority would be a victory for the Cameronmodernisation project, and that the real issue would be whether GB could hold onto those south-east marginals that had stayed with Labour in 2005. If not, Blair's 'New Labour coalition' was dead and the Tories would win next time round. They knew as well as we did that voters in those marginals were the ones who'd been most hostile to GB before he took over in 2007 (mainly because of taxes) and therefore least impressed by the presentational contrast he offered to Tony Blair, which was going down so well in the rest of the country.

It was when voices from the left started saying the same thing that things became tricky. Martin Kettle wrote a highly critical *Guardian* column about GB's prevarication, calling the prospect of an early election an act of 'opportunism and no little vanity'. Many left-wing journalists argued in private that if Labour lost even one seat as a result of that 'vanity', GB would have to resign. I brought this up at a meeting of the 'inner circle', and said surely any working majority for Labour that took us through to a post-Olympics election in 2012 was a triumph compared to where we'd been a year ago. The others round the table looked at me coldly and Ian Austin said: 'They're right – he'd have to resign.'

It seems madness now, but that remained the consensus right up until 5 October, when the final decision was made. And this is where the polls were indeed crucial. Every poll that we ever looked at in those weeks – private or public – said that Labour would win a clear majority. When journalists and the Tories later mocked GB, saying: 'So you're saying you didn't look at the polls, realise you were going to lose, and cancel the election?' he was telling the truth. But the same polls, especially after the Tory conference, said he was going to shed at least a dozen south-east (and Midlands) marginals. And once the consensus took hold that a slimmer majority would be a resignation-worthy outcome, that became reason enough not to go for it.

DEVIL'S ADVOCATES

However, that all seemed a long way off on the weekend of Tory conference (29/30 September), when the inner circle gathered at Chequers for yet another strategy discussion. For most of us, it was our first time there, and Gordon started the day with a tour of the glorious old building. In a way only he could have got away with, Ed Miliband mimicked a Jewish patriarch being shown round his successful grandson's house: 'Nice place you've got here, Gordon, nice bit of real estate.'

We sat around the grand dining table, and Gordon opened things up by saying, 'Right, I want to go round and flush out all the reasons why we shouldn't go for it.' There was silence, eventually broken by Ed Balls: 'Well, just to play devil's advocate…' One after another, those round the table offered desultory arguments against an early election. Douglas: 'Voter registration's going to be a problem – lots of students will be disenfranchised.' Ed Miliband: 'It'll be dark before and after work – lots of people will just stay home rather than vote in the dark.'

Gordon called a halt to the discussion, and moved on to all the reasons we should go for it, receiving a much more enthusiastic response. I made my one contribution to the discussion. 'Well, from a media perspective, I think we've got to think about the reaction if we decide not to go for it now – they'll absolutely slaughter us.' One of the MPs looked down the table at me and said, 'Hold on, the worst possible reason to go for it is what happens if we don't.' There was a murmur of assent. I remember immediately thinking, 'Isn't that the best possible reason to go for it?', but I didn't say it out loud and the moment passed.

LOCATION IS EVERYTHING

One of the cardinal rules of political PR is to make sure you're in direct contact with the person writing the story. That may sound obvious, but too many spin-doctors rely on emails or press releases or getting a story on the newswires, when the art of spin is about talking a journalist through your message and the context, preferably face-to-face so you can be sure they're actually listening.

One of the worst things a politician can do is make an announcement on a regional visit or a trip overseas when the story will be written out of London: a recipe either to be ignored or – to use a technical term – shit-bagged. In August 2006, George Osborne went to Japan and announced that he wanted to build one of their magnetic-levitating train lines back in Britain.

I absolutely destroyed him that day: the history of accidents and fires on mag-levs; the fact it wouldn't have time to get up to top speed on the route Osborne was proposing. I was told by one journalist that Osborne texted him and said: 'What's going on with this story? Why is everyone so down on it?' He said he replied: 'You've just met the Dog' (Mad Dog – rather than McPoison – was my lobby nickname).

When Osborne made his announcement on inheritance tax[12] at the Tory conference, to be paid for by a new levy on non-doms, it was another chance for me to destroy him – and on my specialist subject, too. The sums didn't come close to adding up, and I was confident it would become another example of a panicky Tory Party scoring own goals. But the story was being reported out of Blackpool, by journalists with Tory spin-doctors and the cheers of the conference hall in their ears. I couldn't get a hearing.

The same was true when GB flew to Iraq on 2 October – on the advice of civil servants who wanted to get a visit in before election purdah began. When the Tories wheeled out John Major to complain about the 'cynical timing', a story that should have been covered by the journalists with GB in Iraq became a story written out of Blackpool, with predictable results.

Those two events didn't feel to me like game-changers in themselves – at least at the time – but they did shift the media

---

12 Famously, GB had two options before his last Budget in 2007: one to cut the basic rate of income tax by abolishing the 10 pence rate; the other to cut inheritance tax by allowing married couples to combine their tax-free allowances. This was where the starter process that I've described before could actually work against good decision-making. The income tax proposal was relatively straightforward, whereas every time we looked at the IHT proposal, we came up with new reasons why it might not work: what about recently widowed individuals, what about war widows, how far back could you go if you wanted to make it retrospective, and how much more would it cost. We ended up convincing ourselves that there was too much risk of it unravelling on the day, whereas the income tax proposal was an easier sell. It was the wrong call and October 2007 might have turned out very differently if we'd made the right one.

momentum, and hardened the poll deficit in those crucial south-east marginals. They created the climate for GB to wobble when the moment of decision came.

NEVER PLAY POKER WITH ED BALLS

After GB's return from Iraq, the mood had discernibly shifted. People who had previously been arch-proponents of the early election had started to play devil's advocate more frequently and enthusiastically. It didn't help that some of the MPs GB was listening to were clearly thinking about their own majorities and whether they personally would survive. GB's pollsters were also – to cover their backs – starting to paint worst-case scenarios, all of which ended up with GB resigning after a drastic reduction in Labour's majority.

Throughout that wobbly week, the only strong dissenting voice belonged to Ed Balls. His mantra was that – whatever the polls said now – Labour would wipe the floor with the Tories during the election campaign. 'These guys are amateurs,' he would say of Cameron and Osborne. 'They've never fought a general election before – they don't know what it takes. We'll just say: "Are you really going to trust this pair to run the country? Are you going to take that risk?"'

It was amazing to me that – of all the MPs involved in the decision-making process – only Ed Balls (and to some extent Tom Watson) had any confidence that Labour could *increase* its lead over the course of a campaign and was willing to gamble on that outcome. But as I wrote the other day, and as he demonstrated again in 2010 with his call on the economy, Balls has always been good at calculating the odds and knowing when to bet.[13]

---

13 I myself was very confident (and frankly a bit excited) about the potential election campaign, having not been involved in one before. One of my most treasured pieces of memorabilia is the 'treatment' I wrote for a potential party political broadcast in 2007, which reads as follows (with apologies to *The Day Today*, which inspired it, and to PR professionals who do this stuff for a living):

We open with a milkman on his early-morning rounds in a wealthy suburban street listening to Classic FM playing 'I vow to thee my country'. He waves cheerily at a postman walking the other way. The postman starts whistling 'I vow to thee'.

A mum takes a parcel from him at her door, and keeps la-la-ing the tune in a lovely melodious voice as she and Dad get the kids ready for school, and climb into the family Range Rover. Dad gets out at the station, humming the tune, and gets on board a gleaming new train with other commuters.

An orchestra and male voice choir (humming) take up the tune in the background, as we cut to real footage of trains arriving at stations in London, Manchester, Birmingham, Cardiff, Belfast, Glasgow and Edinburgh, suited commuters pouring off the trains to go to work.

The orchestra and choir soaring now, we cut in quick time across the bright skylines of Britain's cities, then to construction sites, university students walking and cycling, a gleaming new classroom in a primary school, a hospital room with a doctor and nurse showing a smiling elderly patient a gleaming piece of new equipment, two police officers walking through a crowded shopping centre etc.

The orchestra and choir slowing and quietening now as we get to the end of the day: smart young City types laughing in a wine bar; a barmaid pulling a pint of beer in a village pub and laughing with the chaps at the bar; a mum and dad taking excited kids into the new Wembley all lit up in front of them; teenagers dancing and shouting at a concert at the O2.

The orchestra and choir going almost silent, replaced by just a single, vaguely familiar baritone voice humming the tune. Households across the country are going to bed: an elderly woman turns the heat up before getting into bed; the mum we saw earlier looks in on her sleeping kids; the nurse we saw earlier checks that the elderly patient is asleep in the now dark hospital.

We cut to an old building with all the lights off apart from one window. We move at worm's-eye level through a familiar black door, then up carpeted stairs, down a long corridor, deep red carpets, with one room lit up at the end, and the faint humming of the closing bars of 'I vow to thee' growing louder as we move towards the light.

We pan round the door, a sideways shot of Gordon Brown sat at his desk, his red box in front of him, going through papers and signing documents, humming to himself. He finishes the last bar, looks down at the camera, smiles and says: 'Good night.'

Dissolve to black. Captions come up in turn: 'He's working', 'You're working', 'Britain's working', 'Don't let the Tories ruin it'. It might just have worked!

THE LAST WORDS

By Friday 5 October, with Balls away in Yorkshire, the inner circle gathered in Alastair Campbell's old office facing out onto Downing Street heard the latest unchanged poll findings from marginal constituencies, and sat waiting for Gordon to announce the inevitable.

You'd have forgiven him for lashing out in almost every direction round the room, and he was clearly angry at those who'd urged him along at every stage and were now counselling caution, but he was grimly quiet. Finally, he said, 'Right, well, does anyone have anything they want to say?', like the lawyer of a condemned man hoping someone in the courtroom will produce an alibi. Heads bowed. There was silence.

Finally, Bob Shrum cleared his throat. Bob had been in the doghouse since the party conference plagiarism episode, so I admired him for speaking up. 'Well, if the worst comes to the worst, and you only get three more years, there's a lot you can do in three years. Jack Kennedy only had three years.' Gordon didn't look up, didn't look back, and walked out of the room. And that was that.

MEA CULPA, MEA CULPA, MEA MAXIMA CULPA

The media handling of the announcement on the Saturday was nothing short of a catastrophe, and made an already disastrous news story into a total clusterfuck. That is all my fault, although – like a bad workman – I'm going to plead some sub-optimal equipment.

First, there was Gordon. His mood was such that even doing one pre-recorded TV interview with Andrew Marr seemed a massive risk. Asking him to do a press conference or a whole round of interviews could have led to a public meltdown which would probably have forced his resignation and an election anyway. Think his post-Mrs Duffy interview with Jeremy Vine times 1,000.

Second, there was the timing. Every Sunday paper was doing a minimum of four pages of coverage on the impending election decision, with polls and 'will he, won't he ... should he, shouldn't he' columns. The announcement on the Saturday was going to come as a complete surprise to them, and – depending when it broke – might have meant pages or sections having to be pulped, columns having to be rewritten and so on.

The long-term damage that would have done to No. 10's relationship with the Sunday papers would have been huge – potentially irrecoverable – and if there's one thing I'd always sought to avoid in my job, it was the Sunday papers turning hostile to GB. The Sundays have the resources, the journalists, the columnists, the readership, the competitive impulse and the influence over the Sunday broadcast media to kill you politically. What's more, it's too debilitating for a senior politician and their team to spend every weekend firefighting when they should be recharging for the week ahead.

So this was how it was supposed to work. I arranged with Andrew Marr's producer, Barney Jones, on the Friday that Andrew would come in the following afternoon and do the pre-record, so Gordon could explain his decision in his own words and try to look relaxed about it. Nobody in the BBC would be told this was happening until after it had been done, but extracts would be released to all outlets for the Saturday early-evening news.

In the meantime, on Saturday morning, I'd tip off the political editors of all the Sundays that an announcement was coming, on the understanding that this go no further than their editor, news editor and lead columnist so they could reshape their pages, coverage and columns. You might think that is impossibly naive, but those kind of caveated tip-offs are given all the time to newspapers and they tend to respect them, for the obvious reason that they want the same kind of consideration next time round.

Given that the Sundays also had to explain at great length how and why the decision had been taken, I also did what I did best: giving them 'the colour' – who was in the room when; who said what; which room we were in; what GB had for breakfast. That gave me the licence to spin the line that GB's mood had been moving against an election for some time, even before the Tory conference and the shift in the polls; there were worries about voter registration, people having to vote in the dark etc. The desultory devil's advocate lines from Chequers became serious and influential concerns.

Anyway, that was how it was supposed to work. As far as I've pieced it together since, one of the Sundays tipped off Andy Coulson, he tipped off the broadcasters, and all hell broke loose. By the time Marr arrived to do the interview, every camera in the world was outside Downing Street and Adam Boulton, Nick Robinson and co. were spitting tacks down their microphones outside. It created a sense of utter chaos and shambles around what was already a deeply damaging story, although I'll maintain to this day that we were right to avoid permanently pissing off the Sunday papers.

I've no doubt that – like LAPD Officer Karl Hettinger, who surrendered his weapon to two thieves in the Onion Field incident in 1963 and saw his partner shot – my bungling of that day will be taught to young PR professionals for years to come as an example of how not to do things. But the more interesting question to ask them is: how would you have handled it?

DISCOVERING THAT 'YOU' MEANT 'ME'

If you work for someone as driven as Gordon Brown, you accept to some extent that your life will be subsumed to theirs. I was literally at his beck and call twenty-four hours a day, seven days a week, for six years. It didn't matter if I was on holiday, cooking Christmas lunch, at a funeral, or – most grievous of all – watching Arsenal, I'd be expected to drop everything to take his calls, or indeed the media's if there was a story I had to deal with. And I was fine with that. I had no political ambitions, no personal agenda of my own, and my life was about protecting and promoting Gordon, and – by extension, at least as far as I was concerned – the best interests of the Labour Party and the country.

For that reason, I got used – over the years – to hearing a journalist use the word 'you' and assuming they meant Gordon. 'What are you saying about this?' 'How are you reacting?' 'What are you thinking about conference?' meant Gordon, and I was merely a conduit for his words and views. So on a daily basis, I'd work out what issue we might have to deal with, I'd talk it through with Gordon, he'd give me 'the line', and if I agreed it worked, that would become my script.

On fraught days like the cancelled election, or Alistair Darling's 'We're all doomed' interview with Decca Aitkenhead, or the exposure of David Abrahams's dodgy donations, Gordon would be absolutely clear with me and his civil service spokesman what our line was, what the story he wanted written was, and our job – however difficult – was to try to deliver it.

If I'd ever rung a journalist and said, 'This is Gordon's position blah blah blah ... but by the way, here's what I personally think' and said the complete opposite – 'It's all Douglas Alexander's fault' or 'Alistair Darling needs to be sacked' or 'David Triesman's in the frame for this one', not only would I have been failing to get the story Gordon wanted and incurring his wrath in the process, but the journalist concerned would have stopped regarding me as a reliable conduit for Gordon's views.

So when two journalists rang me on Sunday 7 October and said, 'There's a lot of flak coming your way' and 'People are sticking the boot into you quite hard', it took me a while to realise 'you' didn't mean Gordon; it meant 'me'.

'Me?' I kept saying, 'Me? What have I done?'

'Well, accusations that you're briefing against various people for being responsible, but some people are saying that all the media speculation was your fault, and that you're as responsible as anyone.'

'Me? Are you serious? Who's saying that?'

'Well obviously I can't say, but how do you want to respond?'

Looking back, I had the worst possible reaction – I didn't care. I just thought: 'Sod 'em. Idiots. They can say what they like.'

The trouble is if you think like that – if you don't protest the first time you're falsely accused of friendly fire – then: a) people think you're guilty; b) the real guilty party knows they can do what they like and you'll get the blame; c) you start getting the blame for everything no matter how far-fetched; and d) worst of all, you start to think 'I'm as well hung for a sheep as a lamb', and the accusations start to become self-fulfilling, not least when you're under attack yourself.

THE STEEL IN ED MILIBAND'S SOUL

But as apathetic as I might have been to most of that flak, I'll always remember that Sunday sadly as the day I fell out with Ed Miliband. I'd known Ed for eight years. I worked with him on tax policy issues as a civil servant, and when I became Head of Communications at the Treasury in 2003, we travelled the world together with Gordon.

Where Ed Balls was a Gladstone – intimidatingly bright, powerful and demanding to work for – Ed Miliband was indeed a Disraeli – his catchphrase was 'You're a genius'; he'd wear his intelligence behind a self-deprecating veneer; he'd apologise for making you work late and thank you profusely and genuinely for the work you'd done.

When he called me that Sunday, I told him what a joke it was that I was being accused of briefing against him and others. 'But where's it all coming from, Damian?' he said. 'They've got all these details of the meetings we had; that must have come from you.'

'Of course that stuff's from me,' I said, 'that's just the colour – that's harmless – but they're accusing me of doing the lines blaming you and Douglas and Spencer for the whole thing.'

'Well, where's all that coming from, Damian?'

His voice and tone reminded me eerily of Hal, the computer in the film *2001*.

'I don't know, but it's not from me – I'd never brief against you.'

'I don't believe you, Damian,' he said. 'I think you're lying.' It felt like an ice-cold razor had been dragged down my spine.

'Ed, for God's sake, don't say that. I'd never brief against you.'

'That's the trouble, Damian, I don't believe that's true. I think you're lying.'

'Stop saying that, Ed. You can't accuse me of lying. I'm not going to have that.'

'I can't help it, Damian, I think you're a liar.'

'If you keep saying that, you know we're finished, I'm not having that.'

'I don't care, Damian, I think we are finished.'

The call ended. I wandered round the Holloway Road in a daze, went into the Hercules pub and downed three pints in ten minutes, then walked down to the Emirates and watched Arsenal beat Sunderland 3–2 to go top of the league. And again, buoyed by booze and Arsenal's late winner, I had the worst possible reaction to my fallout with Ed Miliband – sod him.

Three years later, after Steve Richards's biography and radio series on Gordon's premiership appeared and repeated the accusation that I'd been responsible for the anti-Ed and anti-Douglas briefings that day, I was called up by a Labour MP – not someone who'd been prominently involved in the 'should we, shouldn't we' discussions – who said: 'I just want to say sorry, you're getting it in the neck again for the briefings that day, and it was me who did them, and I'm sorry for that.'

By that stage I didn't care. In some ways, I'd just had a dose of my own Treasury medicine: I'd been Admiral Bynged – a convenient person to blame, and it wasn't the guilt that mattered, it was the perception that someone close to Gordon (and to Ed Balls) had tried to pin the blame on Ed Miliband and Douglas, allowing them to get some distance from the sinking ship in No. 10 and some victim status with Labour MPs.

But – with the benefit of perspective – I have to admire the steeliness in Ed Miliband. It wouldn't have been easy to tell someone who'd worked loyally for him for eight years that he was finished with them, and to do so in such cold-blooded tones. We saw it again in 2010 when he sacked Nick Brown as Chief Whip. That's not a man who'd struggle with the difficult personnel decisions you face as Prime Minister and, arguably, that's not a man who – if he rather than Gordon had been leader in 2007 – would have wobbled when the moment of decision came.

POSTSCRIPT

You might expect the mood in Downing Street the following week to have been dark, but strangely – almost like a hospital ward – there was a determined cheerfulness amongst the staff, and GB (typically when he blamed himself for a screw-up) was sweetness and light to everyone. It was only over the coming weeks when – with the media in a feeding frenzy, PMQs becoming a weekly humiliation, and a run of terrible ill-fortune or incompetent government depending on your perspective (climaxing in HMRC's loss of the child benefit discs) – that the gloom really set in.

At that stage, much as the current administration must be feeling, it felt that everything that could go wrong was going wrong: GB had lost all credibility with the media and in Parliament, and it was hard to see what would turn it round. And GB himself was deeply wounded: his hard-won reputation for iron will, decisiveness, competence and strategic genius gone overnight.

But I'd like to think that he learned from the experience, and when he had his version of Kennedy's 'Thirteen Days' – with the world facing the complete collapse of the banking system and the descent into economic meltdown and anarchy that would have resulted, and every other world leader not just wobbling but panicking – it was Gordon who knew what they all had to do, and had the iron will and decisiveness to persuade them.

If he had gone for the election in 2007 and been forced to resign afterwards with Labour's majority reduced, he wouldn't have been there the following year to steer Britain and the world through that crisis. So who's to say it wasn't the right decision after all?

JIMMY SAVILE'S KNIGHTHOOD: THE CIVIL SERVICE REARGUARD

9 OCTOBER 2012

'M GOING TO take a wild guess on something, based on three reasonable assumptions and a bit of background knowledge:

1. I don't think there's any way *The Sun* would launch a front-page campaign to strip Jimmy Savile of his knighthood – along with a detailed description of the law change required to make it happen – unless No. 10 had given them some kind of nod that they were sympathetic to the proposal.

2.   Hence I don't think it was any kind of accident or a case of being under-briefed when David Cameron told *Daybreak* this morning that 'We have in Britain something called the forfeiture committee … that looks at whether honours should be rescinded, and I'm sure that they will obviously want to do their jobs.'

3.   Equally, I don't think it was a cock-up that despite the PM's words, a Cabinet Office spokesman then said that the question did not arise since the knighthood became defunct upon Savile's death, thus making Cameron look rather foolish – something *The Times* captured in its juxtaposition of the two headlines.

So, what is going on? Here's where some background knowledge may be helpful.

The idea of awarding posthumous honours has been around for many years, most notably with the campaign for Bobby Moore to receive the knighthood that many of his surviving 1966 peers received in the years after his death. After all, posthumous honours already exist, but only in cases where members of the armed forces or emergency services are killed while engaged in acts of great bravery.

The last great effort to introduce posthumous honours was led by myself and Ian Austin MP, with the support of Cabinet Office minister Tom Watson in 2008/9.

We seized on the campaign by the Holocaust Educational Trust (HET) to see honours awarded to – excuse the phrase – those British 'Heroes of the Holocaust' who had helped Jewish people to escape the concentration camps, usually at great risk to themselves, while working in Britain's embassies in Germany and Occupied Europe. In many cases, their heroic deeds had gone unknown and unrecognised in their own lifetimes, a classic example of why posthumous honours are required.

To be honest, my own interest in posthumous honours was primarily football-related, thinking about all those managerial legends whose achievements in the game would have undoubtedly brought them knighthoods in today's honours system, but who had died unrecognised: Herbert Chapman, Jock Stein, Bob Paisley and Brian Clough, to name four obvious candidates.

We were encouraged in our efforts by Gordon, who added his own *cause célèbre* to ours: he felt that British society owed it to Alan Turing to recognise his great service and the appalling way he had been treated, not just by apologising to him in the House of Commons, as Gordon did, but by giving him the knighthood that he had deserved in his lifetime.

Usually, if the combined weight of Gordon, Tom, Ian and I wanted something done, we could get it done, but on this occasion, we met an immovable object: the combined strength of the civil service and the palace establishment. They were not having it, not under any circumstances – but once we got them at least to explain their reasoning, it was one of the most memorable policy ding-dongs I ever experienced.

We went back and forth over a period of weeks: they would list ten reasons why it couldn't possibly happen; I'd challenge all of them; they'd concede two but insist on the remaining eight;

I'd challenge again, and so on, like boxers going toe-to-toe seeing who would get exhausted first.

We cannot impose honours on people who do not have the opportunity to refuse them.
But you do it for deceased police officers and soldiers – no one asks them – and in any case, why not just ask their surviving families?

We cannot second-guess the judgements made by honours committees in previous years who chose not to honour these individuals.
But some of them – like the Holocaust Heroes – died without anyone knowing what they'd done; and some of them – like Chapman and Stein – dropped dead in the middle of their careers; there wasn't time to honour them.

We cannot make judgements now based on today's criteria and standards and apply them retrospectively to previous eras when different criteria and standards applied.
If you mean that Alan Turing couldn't get a knighthood because he was a homosexual, then are you really saying we should stand by that?

We only have a set number of honours to award each year; if you want to give some to dead people, you're going to have to exclude deserving living people.
Cobblers – just set aside ten extra honours per year, and choose the most deserving posthumous candidates each time.

To whom is Her Majesty supposed to make the award?
Are you serious? You already make awards to half the recipients of the Victoria Cross without them physically receiving it – stop being daft.

How far back are we supposed to go? Do you want to propose that Boadicea is made a Dame?
Again, let's not be daft. But if you want a cut-off point, let's go back to 1917, when the honours system as we know it now came into being.

I nearly had them beaten. But ultimately they fell back on two incontrovertible arguments:

1. HM The Queen doesn't want to do it, and if the PM feels so strongly about it, he will need to take it up with her personally (I'm not sure they ever consulted HM The Queen, but were quite happy to use her name anyway); and

2. All this is a nonsense anyway, since to be awarded a knighthood is really to be made a member of the Order of the Bath etc. You cease to be a member when you die; it follows that dead people cannot be made members.

Ultimately, the dismissive way in which the second reason was presented meant that the first would never be challenged; neither Gordon nor any other PM was going to make an eejit of themselves by proposing the change if 'nonsense' was going to feature in the first line of HM The Queen's response.

Gordon, Ian and Tom settled for the compromise of creating a special new medal for the 'Heroes of the Holocaust', which was duly awarded to several individuals nominated by the HET, and only I was left to fulminate about the establishment rearguard that had denied Jock Stein and Brian Clough their due recognition. Not for the first time, eh, gents?

Now we step into the present day, when *The Sun* launches its campaign on Jimmy Savile at Tory Party conference with a nod and a wink from the political team at No. 10 (I'm assuming). David Cameron, who had the successful experience of leaning on the Honours Forfeiture Committee over Fred Goodwin, spies an easy win on a populist issue, and effectively throws his weight behind *The Sun*, only to get totally shit-bagged by his own civil servants in the Cabinet Office.

Why? Because they recognise that if they yield to the campaign on Jimmy Savile, then they concede the principle that knighthoods exist after death, and the only real, incontrovertible argument that they had left the last time this was debated would be instantly destroyed. That's why they've leapt straight to that argument in their response this afternoon.

Does any of this matter? Lots of people will rightly say that the PM, civil servants, special advisers and the palace should have better things to do than bestowing knighthoods on dead people, or indeed withdrawing them. Lots of people will also rightly say it's another example of how the whole honours system is a discredited anachronism. But, hell, I bet those same people are more likely to have a discussion about it in the pub tonight than about

George Osborne's 'Swap your Tea Breaks for Tax Breaks' scheme, or whatever it was called.

And there's another reason it matters. I never saw a civil service rearguard like the one on posthumous honours in thirteen years in government, not even over Dawn Primarolo's VAT cut on tampons (and that was some rearguard, I can tell you). And there was something about it that smacked of the civil service/palace establishment saying to the grubby politicos: 'Hands off, plebs, this belongs to us: these are our knighthoods; we decide where they go; and we're not sharing them with any dead code-breakers or bloody football managers.'

And I'm guessing that – if the civil service felt strongly about this when it was just a case of a behind-closed-doors discussion with me about the pros and cons – they must be blooming furious at the idea of being bounced into it by the PM at a political party conference to get a cheap campaign win for News International.

Or maybe I'm just bitter. But I bet David Cameron and *The Sun* know the feeling this afternoon. More power to your elbow, chaps – that rearguard is cracking – and they won't dare plead opposition from HM The Queen in this case.

FLIGHT 571:
THE MIRACLE IN THE ANDES

12 OCTOBER 2012

O N THIS DAY forty years ago, a rugby team set off from Montevideo in Uruguay for their second tour of Chile. They were accompanied by two dozen friends and family helping to pay for the charter of the Uruguayan Air Force plane.

After bad weather halted their first attempt to cross the Andes, they tried again the next day. Flying in thick cloud above the mountains, the pilots of Flight 571 got their calculations horribly wrong. Descending into what they thought was Chile, they instead emerged in the middle of the mountains.

Both wings were ripped off the plane, and one sliced off the tail. The fuselage crashed up the mountainside, crushing the passengers inside, and came to a halt almost more than 12,000 feet above sea level, in sub-zero temperatures. Twelve passengers and crew were killed in the crash and its immediate aftermath. Thirty-three remained alive, some with terrible injuries.

What happened to that group of thirty-three over the next three months became one of the twentieth century's most dramatic and haunting tales of hardship, courage and survival, a story of brotherhood tested under the most extraordinary circumstances. There was no one leader. Some individuals who initially rallied the group eventually succumbed to despair. Others overcame deep personal grief to become heroes when the time came to seek rescue.

It is a story of faith. All on board the plane were Catholics, and for many, it was their faith and prayer that sustained their hope, and which enabled them to transform in their minds what the world would describe as cannibalism into a sacred act of sacrifice and communion.

It is above all a story about the triumph of the human spirit; the determination to survive. The group regularly had to deal with the crushing of their hopes: the news coming through via radio that all searches had been called off; the avalanche that claimed the lives of many who had survived the crash. But no matter how bad things got, their sheer will to live triumphed.

Shortly after the remaining survivors were finally rescued, the father of one of those who had not returned wrote an open letter to the newspapers, saying:

We invite every citizen of our country to spend some minutes in meditation on the immense lesson of solidarity, courage and discipline which has been left to us by these boys in the hope that it will serve us all to overcome our mean egotism and petty ambitions, and our lack of interest for our brothers.

Amen to that.

WHY DAVE NEEDS ARTIE,
PAULA & BEVERLY

22 OCTOBER 2012

DOES DAVID CAMERON believe in karma? If so, he must wonder whether the current state of his premiership is some cosmic payback for the events of five years ago, when it was Gordon Brown experiencing one 'worst week ever' after another, and Cameron leading the gleeful taunts.

The Election That Never Was, the feuding of Gordon's inner circle, Anthony Seldon's *Blair Unbound* biography, the Scottish elections fiasco, the ongoing row over 'British jobs for British workers', another foot-and-mouth leak from the Pirbright laboratory, the loss of the child benefit discs, David Abrahams's dodgy donations, the rows over Wendy Alexander's and Peter Hain's undeclared donations. Over a two-month period, every time we thought it couldn't get worse, it got worse, and the demands from the party's so-called grey beards for someone to 'get a grip' grew ever louder.

Now David Cameron must know the feeling. Unfortunately for him, he seems to be lurching into some of the same mistakes that – with the luxury of considerable hindsight – I can see that Gordon made in that period, prolonging the vicious circle of bad headlines and misguided responses.

First, he – like Gordon – is trying to announce his way out of the crisis, going into each Sunday morning and each PMQs with a fresh attempt to get on top of the news agenda with some random, focus-group-designed announcement. At its very least, this is a waste of potentially good stories and speeches which should be held back until there's a chance of them being heard; worse, it leads to the bungled announcement of half-baked policies, like the fuel bills balls-up; and worse still, it leads to ridiculous headlines like 'Cameron: Now Mug A Hoodie'.

Second, he and his team are fighting forest fires with buckets of sand, when what they need is proper firebreaks, i.e. moments when the pre-existing political news agenda is suspended (or at least turned into a backdrop) while another issue or event comes to the fore. It could be a Budget, a Queen's Speech, a trip to Washington, a Defence White Paper: anything that obliges the political media to focus their attention elsewhere for a few days, not least – to put it crudely – if they want to get an exclusive preview. So where are the coalition's firebreaks? The only one I can see on the horizon is George Osborne's Autumn Statement on 5 December; that feels a long time away.

Third, and not for the first time, David Cameron is coming across as a one-man band. He is trying to do too much himself, and is over-exposed in the media. Why is he making a crime speech in the first place? Why is he announcing energy policy? These are the acts of a PM who feels a personal pressure – but also a personal responsibility – to turn things around. If he was on good form, this might be an OK thing, but I fear what political insiders view as robust media performances come across to the public as irritable. Plus, when the PM takes all the load on himself, the Cabinet switch off and start watching comedy DVDs in first class carriages without thinking about how that looks.

Fourth, the one vital antidote to any temporary mood of crisis is the sense that the person in charge has bigger and more important things to worry about. Obviously the main thing that will determine the next election is the state of the economy and the deficit, but to the extent that the PM projects himself as being '100 per cent focused' on those issues, it tends to be about the next set of jobs and growth figures, or what's happened with the deficit since the election, not about the really big picture. If I was him, I would immerse myself in the details of the Basel III bank regulations and forecasts of Chinese commodity inventories, and adopt an air – or, even better, adopt the reality – of constant concern about what will happen to the world economy in 2014.

Finally, and most importantly, we hear the dread call for 'fresh blood' in No. 10. There are two phrases that every former Gordon

Brown staffer got used to hearing when he couldn't hide his exasperation with them any longer. The first – delivered slowly and usually punctuated with a pounding fist on the back of a chair – was: 'Too. Many. Mistakes.' The second – delivered in a strangled growl, usually at the person he wanted to murder on the spot – was: 'I NEED NEW PEOPLE.'

So it is we hear the demands for David Cameron to get rid of Andrew Cooper and Craig Oliver or rein in Sir Jeremy Heywood, and we can be fairly sure that David Cameron and George Osborne are discussing exactly those issues, not least as they ponder how to fill the gaps that are being left in the communications operation with the departures of Steve Field and Gabby Bertin.

It is always tempting to think that your problems will be solved by hiring new or better people, and that is exactly the route that Gordon went down after his two months from hell in 2007.

Not only did that not work for Gordon, it proved positively damaging, as the new staff struggled to find their feet in an atmosphere of rolling crisis management, and as morale amongst his pre-existing team of civil servants and special advisers collapsed to rock-bottom. And if there's one thing you can't afford when you're handling crises, it's half your people not knowing what they're supposed to do and the other half not feeling motivated to do it.

I don't know whether David Cameron needs new people or not, but I do know this: the people are not the most important thing – it's the function he gives them. And that brings me to the three people who can save Dave's premiership.

If you want to learn about handling crises in government, you shouldn't watch *The West Wing* or *The Thick of It*; just watch *The Larry Sanders Show*. Almost every episode tells the story of how a group of people, whatever the dysfunctional behind-the-scenes turmoil, manage to present a successful show at the end of the day. And besides Larry – who is obviously Cameron right down to the luxuriant hair – there are three individuals who are essential to making every show a success, all with distinct responsibilities, all comparable to roles in Downing Street.

Paula (Janeane Garofalo) is not just the talent-booker; she is the talent – the brains and creativity of the show, but rooted in the real world of what will work and what the audience will like. She is also the show's strategic planner, spotting problems and filling holes, whether days in advance or minutes before show-time. In No. 10, she would be in charge of the strategic grid, planning the firebreaks, spotting the opportunities, stopping the screwups, and ensuring the talent from elsewhere in the Cabinet gets a chance to shine.

Beverly (Penny Johnson) runs Larry's life. She manages his time, energy and mood, deciding who he needs to see and what he needs to do. Nobody else has this control, not even Larry's wives, and it is not shared with anyone. In No. 10, she would be the PM's gatekeeper, diary manager and closest confidante, and, crucially, she would have the power to tell the civil servants, press officers and advisers who all want a piece of his time and energy when they can and cannot have it.

Artie (Rip Torn) has one job: making the whole operation work, ensuring that when the curtain goes up, the audience sees an entertaining, professional show and a smiling, relaxed host. He saves Larry from the stuff he doesn't have to deal with, and deals brutally with anyone trying to undermine Larry or disrupt the show. In No. 10, he'd be the person who'd ensure everyone else was doing their job and nothing was distracting the PM from doing his. Like it or not, Andrew Mitchell would have been gone in five minutes with an Artie in the room.

At present, David Cameron looks to me like he's in one of those *Larry Sanders* episodes where the network is trying to make him change his style, or where he feels he needs to bring in new writers, or where he's worried about some rival presenter stealing his show or being upstaged by one of the guests. Worse still, his Cabinet and many of his officials and advisers are acting like a bunch of Hanks and Phils, worried about their own interests and futures, not about protecting his.

If he wants to shake up his personnel in No. 10 and he feels that is crucial in order to get out of the current crisis mode, then he first needs to establish what jobs need doing. He needs to create and then fill the roles of an Artie, a Paula and a Beverly, whether that means giving more power to existing staff members or bringing in new people.

In his time in Downing Street, Gordon didn't have any individual playing any of those roles. Not even Sue Nye enjoyed the exclusive power over his time and energy that a proper Beverly would have; he lacked a consistent Paula figure; and he never came close to establishing an Artie.

If David Cameron sorts out those roles, then things like planning firebreaks, avoiding botched announcements, focusing on the big picture and getting the rest of the Cabinet to raise their game will become that much easier. And, most importantly, it will allow him to get back to presenting himself as a relaxed, confident, natural Prime Minister. With great hair.

DOWNING STREET DOES
NEED NEW PEOPLE

4 NOVEMBER 2012

THE TWO MOST important civil servants in No. 10 are the PM's official spokesman and the PM's principal private secretary. One runs his press office; the other runs his private office. Put another way, one controls what the PM thinks, says and does publicly; the other controls his diary and the work he does behind closed doors.

If those two offices are not run fluently and coherently, Downing Street cannot function and the PM cannot govern effectively. There are of course one or two other things and people that affect the successful functioning of the government, but unless you have excellent individuals in the roles of PMOS and PPS, the battle is already lost.

So even though the news has gone largely unreported, it's hugely important that Jean-Christophe Gray – widely known as JC Gray[14] – has been appointed as the new PMOS, in which role he will give twice-daily official briefings to the parliamentary press, speaking *ex cathedra* on behalf of David Cameron and the government.

It's an immensely tough role, in which you're never more than one misplaced phrase or unintended admission away from causing a media storm. Too many of those and you won't last long, but go in the other direction – know nothing, say nothing, refuse to confirm the truth or even answer your phone – and you will lose all respect and trust. That's fine if you just want to get through each day, but not if you want to help the PM survive when he's next at the epicentre of a shitquake.

JC will not be fazed by difficult days, having managed the Treasury press office during tough periods under Alistair Darling and George Osborne. But more importantly, he has two key characteristics that will stand him in good stead:

---

14 A now forgotten fact: JC Gray is only called JC Gray because of Gordon Brown's total inability to say difficult names. He tried several times to get the hang of saying 'Jean Christophe' when barking out instructions to the new recruit in his private office, before the solution of using 'JC' was suggested to him instead. To avoid confusion, everyone else started referring to Jean Christophe as 'JC' as well, and that became his name. There but for the grace of God went we all. Shortly afterwards, another new recruit – the wonderful Rita Patel, now Mrs Phil French – joined the private office and, having been warned about JC's experience, she was determined not to be similarly re-named. So when Gordon introduced her happily as 'Ruth' to a large gathering of external businesspeople on her first day in the job, she shouted at him, 'It's Rita, Chancellor, RITA!' I'd like to say that he coolly replied, 'OK Rita, but it's not Chancellor, it's Gordon,' but I think he was too taken aback. He never got her name wrong again, though.

He's got integrity. When he was working in Gordon Brown's private office and I was the Treasury's Head of Communications, JC told me that he'd struck up a friendship with a journalist and was planning to invite her round for dinner. Was this OK? When I next saw him, he looked like someone had shot his dog. How did the date go? 'Well, it was going really well,' he said, 'but then she started talking about the pressure she was under at work, having to find out what was happening with council tax revaluation, and asked whether that had crossed my desk … So I asked her to leave.' You did what?! 'Well I was very nice about it, but I said it was best we left it there.' I may be wrong, but that kind of reaction is not the mark of a man who would ever mislead a journalist or deny something he knew to be true.

He's also a professional. He'll get flustered on occasions but he'll never shirk his job, let the pressures get to him, or be flippant about the power he holds. On the day of Budget 2011, I made my annual 'mystery shopper' call to the Treasury press office, and hit the jackpot, being referred to JC himself. Affecting a suitable accent, I said I was the beer correspondent for the *Huddersfield Examiner*, and was furious about the abolition of tax relief for Mathers' Black Beer (a precursor of the bigger and more damaging changes HMRC slipped past the keeper in Budget 2012). JC corpsed. I could hear him desperately stifling the giggles as I thundered on – with genuine conviction – about the impact on local brewing heritage. 'Are ya laffin', lad?' I asked. He composed himself and gave a beautifully crafted and sensitively phrased explanation for the change. Almost as impressive as his recovery and his answer was the fact that he handled the call himself; a less consummate professional would have thought it was beneath him and referred it to HMRC.

But – as well suited as JC may be to the role – there's a more important issue to address about his appointment. It continues a remarkable recent hegemony over the PMOS and PPS roles by individuals who have graduated from senior roles either in the Chancellor's private office or the Treasury press office – or, in JC's case, both.

The current PPS – appointed earlier this year – is Chris Martin, a former Treasury Head of Communications. For the previous thirteen years, the role of PPS had been held by graduates of Ken Clarke's or Gordon Brown's Treasury private office: Jeremy Heywood (twice), Ivan Rogers, Tom Scholar and James Bowler. The exception in that period was Oliver Robbins, but he was as central to Gordon Brown's Treasury operation as any of the others.

As for the PMOS, the hegemony is more short-lived but now seemingly entrenched. Since 2007, the role has gone from Michael 'The Sheik' Ellam to Steve 'Jonatton Yeah?' Field, both former Treasury heads of communication and masters of the PMOS art, and now to JC Gray. The exception in that period was Simon Lewis, a rare outsider, who served for less than a year at the tail-end of the Labour government.

There is one way to look at all this.

You could argue that, since the Treasury has traditionally had the pick of the best fast-stream recruits to the home civil service and the best of those will usually end up in the most important

Treasury positions, then their further ascendance to the top jobs in No. 10 is simply a case of cream rising to the top.

You could also argue that there is no better training for those No. 10 jobs than their equivalent posts in the Treasury, and that the preference for Treasury types reflects the current centrality of the economy to No. 10's work. Whereas with Ivan Rogers, Ollie Robbins and Jeremy Heywood, Tony Blair was poaching Gordon Brown's talent, it is now a case of No. 10's chief strategist, George Osborne, recommending people he knows are up to the job.

But there's another way to look at it.

If, every time there's a vacancy in the PMOS or PPS roles, No. 10 continues drawing on the same narrow field of Treasury candidates, all themselves drawing on similar working experiences, you do risk ending up with a certain homogeneity in the way that the jobs are approached.

And like all narrow gene pools, the effects are multiplied the longer the cycle is unbroken. Given that interviewers tend to select the candidate who most resembles themselves, the fact that most of the individuals I've mentioned recruited each other at various points reinforces that trend, as does the fact that they all came through the same brutal selection process to become fast-stream civil servants in the first place.

Again, given that these individuals are generally the best and brightest Whitehall has to offer, you might argue this is no bad thing. And having myself benefited from this process, I'm hardly in a position to criticise it. However, like all the others, I'm white, male and heterosexual, with a degree from Oxbridge. When I was appointed as the Treasury's Head of Communications in 2003, all seven people involved in my interview process (bar Edinburgh-educated Gordon) were the same.

The Treasury recently completed its 2012 recruitment process for new 'policy advisers', specifying the minimum requirement of a 2:1 degree. The blurb says: 'We want to do everything we can to ensure that we reflect the society we serve', but while the recruitment forms, tests and interviews will be daunting to many candidates, they'll be routine to many others thanks to entrance applications to grammar school, private school or Oxbridge.

The Treasury's standard application form for more senior jobs contains a sequence of three sections for 'Higher Education', 'Subject of Postgraduate Research (if any)', and 'Professional Qualifications'. These are not 'mandatory fields' but it would take a particularly confident soul to leave them blank and carry on in good heart with the rest of their application, and a particularly wise Treasury manager to carry on reading it with an open mind.

None of this means the Treasury, and by extension No. 10, is necessarily recruiting the wrong people to the most important posts, but we do have to ask what they're missing out on by effectively excluding the vast majority of the civil service, not to mention 99.99 per cent of the entire working population, from the reckoning.

And that matters if you assume, as I do, that there are a huge number of highly intelligent, brilliantly creative, politically astute individuals in Britain, with the same integrity and professionalism as a JC Gray, who would never even get their foot in the Treasury's door – let alone have the chance to rise to the most senior positions – because they did not go to university, or because they are unable to present themselves as a 'Treasury type' at interview.

I grew up with friends who started work in the City without A levels or degrees in the 1990s; they would make brilliant Treasury advisers on finance or trade, but would never get a look in. I know journalists from my time in government whose only qualification is shorthand but who would never have let the pasty tax into the Budget. And, during my period in the education and charity sectors, I've met exceptional people who absolutely *should* be advising on child welfare policy rather than some 21-year-old graduate from Peterhouse.

Some of the most important work being done on politics at the moment is by Labour MPs Jon Trickett and Gloria De Piero and Lib Dem activist Louise Shaw. From different perspectives, they're all looking at what kind of people are attracted to a career in politics in the first place, which of them are able to get started, and how those with alternative backgrounds, family lives, emotional needs and income levels (or a simple lack of know-how or contacts) are put off or weeded out.

Jon Trickett has made the point that 91 per cent of those MPs returned at the 2010 election went to university, and of the 9 per cent who did not, we can also note that only the Tories' Patrick McLoughlin and the excellent Grant Shapps now attend either the Cabinet or shadow Cabinet. Where is Labour's next Alan Johnson or the Lib Dems' next Paddy Ashdown? That is precisely what Jon, Gloria and Louise are looking to change, but it's an uphill struggle.

By comparison, widening the field of civil servants we recruit to staff our government offices and fill the most important roles in the Treasury and No. 10 should *not* be so hard. It just requires the Jeremy Heywoods, Chris Martins and JC Grays of the world to recognise – as I have, with the benefit of some external perspective – that, when the time comes to find their own successors, they need to add some fresh blood to the family.

The Treasury's 'policy adviser' recruitment blurb says: 'HM Treasury believes a diverse workforce makes a positive impact on what we can achieve.' Right you are, chaps, let's see you do something about it.

'IS LITTLE NELL DEAD?'
– NOT ON THIS EVIDENCE

28 NOVEMBER 2012

F OR A POLICY geek like me, who spent three years in charge of policy on alcohol duties, hearing that the government was publishing proposals on a minimum unit price (MUP) today felt like being part of the mob at New York Harbour waiting for the arrival of the final chapters of *The Old Curiosity Shop* to see if Little Nell had died.

Having driven through my own seemingly radical reform of the alcohol tax system in 2002, introducing progressive beer duty (a halving of the duty rate paid by small brewers), and seen the explosion in British microbreweries that followed in the decade after, I imagined the civil servants sweating all morning over the impact of these changes.

And as I said on Twitter this morning, the questions for me were how on earth the government could enforce a MUP except through taxation, and what the consequences would be for Britain's drinks industry and consumption habits if it did attempt to impose a 45 pence minimum of excise duty (or duty plus VAT) per unit of alcohol sold?

Opening the consultation document earlier, I was giddy with excitement and trepidation about how they'd solved this conundrum: how could they enforce the MUP except through means that would cause political, industry and consumer chaos? And the answer is: Ummm, they haven't.

There was not a word about enforcement of the MUP (or the related ban on multi-buy offers) in the main consultation document, but turn to 'Impact Assessment A', and we find the following extraordinary 'interim assumptions':

In the 350-odd licensing authorities in England and Wales, on average responsible for almost 500 licensed premises each, it is intended that there will be ONE individual (either local government, police or trading standards – yet to be determined which) spending two hours per week enforcing the new rules. The total cost of enforcement is therefore estimated to be circa £500,000 per year.

For the MUP, we then get this line:

> Enforcement authorities will need to check product prices against
> the MUP and would only expect to do so when there has been

a representation to the enforcing authority which suggests that premises may be in breach of their licence conditions. We expect that enforcement officers will only choose to check alcohol products that are considered to be very low-cost and random sample products if necessary.

Similarly, for multi-buy products, we get this:

Enforcement authorities would need to check that products or promotions falling within the scope of the ban had been removed. We expect that enforcement officers will only choose to do so where there has been a representation to the enforcing authority which suggests that a premises may be in breach of their licensing conditions, although they may also choose to randomly sample products or promotions if necessary.

So let's get this straight. The enforcement of this major flagship reform depends on people complaining to their local authority that the off-licence at the end of the street is selling alcohol at below 45 pence per unit, or selling packs of six lagers at a discount price compared to the cost of six on their own.

Does anyone spot a flaw in that plan? If the same off-licence had a reputation for selling booze or cigarettes to underage kids, then not only would the offence be clear-cut to most locals, but the chances of them being reported would be reasonably good.

But the idea that shopkeepers who have the temerity to offer their wares at discount prices will routinely be dobbed in by their customers (or indeed fellow shopkeepers) is right up there with the notion that homeowners should report builders and plumbers who offer them a cash price for a job.

Of course, the big supermarkets and off-licence chains won't have much choice but to comply because their prices are centrally set; and most pubs, clubs and restaurants won't be affected; but according to the Home Office's own consultation document, that leaves at least 56,149 small and micro-sized off-trade premises where the government is relying on some form of citizen-led enforcement.

As a result of these measures, those places might take down the signs in their windows offering six cans of Stella for a fiver so as not to attract the attention of any passing busybodies, but does anyone think that means the offers themselves will disappear? Especially for locals who've been using those same off-licences and corner shops, and enjoying those deals, for years.

In fact, given the big supermarkets will no longer be able to offer large discount prices and multi-buy offers, those small shops should see an increase in business – the same shops which are (compared to the necessarily stringent standards of a Tesco or Sainsbury's) less choosy about the age of those they sell to, what time they start or stop serving booze, and whether they serve people who are already hammered.

In short, the enforcement regime set out today will not work, and could prove a tad counter-productive. Now the government surely aren't stupid. Whoever wrote that impact assessment must have realised it sounded hopelessly detached from reality. So what's the real game?

I come back to what I said at the outset. The *only* way this policy can be sensibly enforced is through taxation. The *only* way it can be made secure from legal challenge on competition grounds is through taxation. The *only* way it will ever be introduced in practice is through taxation. As for the explanations given in 'Impact Assessment A' as to why it's not being done through taxation, they are so thin that a more cynical man would think they were designed to be overcome.[15]

So I'm prepared to predict that either today's measures (the MUP and multi-buy ban specifically) are introduced as proposed, and then widely ignored by half the population, like the laws on littering or seat-belts in the back seat. Or more likely, the government will conclude that, after due consideration and consultation, they've decided to implement it through taxation.

And, at that point, for the reasons described in my earlier piece on this subject, all hell will break loose.

As McBride predicted, the proposals for minimum unit pricing were dropped in July 2013 after this consultation process.

---

15 For example, we're told that 'a rise in alcohol duty would affect all types of alcohol products, including the most expensive products' whereas 'a MUP is intended to specifically target the sale of cheap alcohol products'. Erm, a minimum duty rate (or duty plus VAT rate) of 45 pence per unit would make not a blind bit of difference to the price of 'the most expensive products', whereas it would jack up the price of all reasonably priced beer and cider and cheaper bottles of wine. We're also told that 'there is no requirement for retailers to pass through higher duties into prices, so higher duties will not automatically raise the price of cheap alcohol'. Erm, the Home Office can pull the other one if they're arguing retailers would be able or willing to absorb a 45 pence per unit duty rate, rather than passing it on to consumers.

PARADISE REGAINED
OR DAMNATION POSTPONED?

5 DECEMBER 2012

I GOT THAT AUTUMN Statement totally wrong. Besides the prospect of no further micro-tinkering with the tax system – which everyone could forecast – my other confident predictions were as follows:

1. George Osborne would suck up the terrible numbers on growth and borrowing, accept he would miss his fiscal targets, get all the bad news out of the way, write it off as a rubbish year, and play the long game; and

2. He wouldn't do any big-ticket measures on the grounds there is no point wasting good announcements on a bad news day, or doing anything controversial to compound that bad news.

On both counts, I was totally wrong.

He couldn't do much about the bad growth forecasts, but he's pulled out all the stops to make the deficit and debt figures less dire, including some accounting tricks which would impress Derren Brown let alone Gordon, and as a result has stayed on the same golf course as his fiscal targets.

And he's made a valiant, and potentially successful, effort to wipe the numbers off the news with some very big-ticket announcements on infrastructure, fuel duty, personal allowances and business taxes, paid for by some massive plus column *dei ex machine* (£3.5 billion from the 4G spectrum sale in Year One; £3.1 billion from the Swiss government in Year Two; and £2.4 billion from his fellow ministers' budgets in Year Three), coupled with the ongoing war of accretion against welfare recipients.

Is it all credible? The genius of today's statement (or the foolishness, depending on your perspective) is that we won't know for months. These aren't measures which will unravel by the weekend like the last Budget, and they've been carefully chosen with that in mind.

So we could look back and say this was the day when George Osborne restored his strategic reputation and put himself back on the path to No. 10 with a brilliantly designed set of measures to get on top of the worst set of numbers he ever had to face.

Or we could look back and say this was the day he departed from reality, missed the chance to draw a line under his *annus horribilis*, and thus guaranteed that when the numbers are even worse next time, and his credibility is exhausted, it'll be Goodnight Gideon.

Which will it be? I'm not predicting anything after today. Except this.

If George Osborne goes down, Robert Chote is going with him. Why? For me, the most significant line in the whole Autumn Statement document – because it will be the first big test of its credibility – is at Paragraph 2.43: 'Following … independent analysis of the likely valuation of [4G] spectrum receipts by the OBR, the receipts will be reflected … at £3.5 billion.'

That £3.5 billion – not a rough projection but a figure now banked in the public finances – is what allowed the Chancellor to say that borrowing was falling this year; it's what allowed him to do a billion quid of fiscal loosening for each of the following three years and claim that the package was fiscally neutral overall. It's a hell of a bet, and it's Chote who made it.

We'll find out in March if he was right or not.

In the event, the 4G spectrum sale in February 2013 raised just £2.3 billion.

THE UNEMPLOYMENT FIGURES: A TAXMAN'S VIEW

12 DECEMBER 2012

'M A GREAT believer in the old adage that if you want to know what's really happening to the economy, ask the taxman. So when I met one of my old pals from HMRC recently, I asked him what was going on with unemployment. Why are the recent figures so good when other economic data is so weak, and when the Job Programme doesn't seem to be doing anything? This is what he said:

> So imagine you're some bloke on disability benefits or JSA, but
> you also sit and mind your sister's flower stall a couple of hours

each day and drive a mini-cab on a Friday night to get some extra cash, but most of the time you're just sat at home or in the pub. Then you get told you need to do three weeks' unpaid work in Tesco to see whether you're fit for work, so you can't earn your cash or sit in the pub. So what are you going to do? You'll tell the Job Centre it's alright, I've managed to get some part-time work and carry on as normal. They lose their benefits but get tax credits instead, so there's not a lot of net gain for the Revenue. And they're not doing any work that they weren't doing before so there's no benefit for GDP. So all round, it's good for the unemployment figures, but not much else.

I've no idea how accurate or typical that scenario is, but I thought it was an interesting perspective, and it would explain a few things.

WHITHER THE GRID?

13 JANUARY 2013

THERE WAS ONE passage in the *Sunday Times*'s exposé of
Steve Hilton's Stanford lecture which told me everything
about the problems the government is currently facing.
According to the report, Hilton dramatically produced a 1-foot
high bundle of paper for his audience representing four days' worth
of documents circulated to Cabinet committees. He then said:
'It just shows you the scale of what you're up against in trying to
control these things. The idea that a couple of political advisers
read through all this and spot things that are bad, things that are
contradictory, is just inconceivable.'

And he's right, which is precisely why a system has been in

place since 1997 which means they don't have to. The 'grid system' initiated by New Labour – transferred from their 1997 election campaign – is commonly considered to be a news management tool, with a series of announcements plotted to dominate each day's coverage and provide occasional cover to bury bad news.

However, its far more important role was doing precisely what Hilton says is impossible: giving political advisers an easily digestible paper (no more than twenty to thirty pages long) containing the key elements of every government announcement or external news item coming up for the next fortnight.

The 'grid' itself was simply an aide-memoire version of this longer document, with each announcement arranged in order of importance and general subject area for each of the next fourteen days on two A4 sheets of paper, with the emerging grids for the next two months added on to give a longer-term view.

This 'Upcoming Business' document would be circulated by No. 10's Strategic Communications Unit each Thursday evening, and would then form the basis of a Friday morning meeting to go through each item in the grid line by line.

At different times under the Labour government, these meetings were chaired by Alastair Campbell, Ed Miliband (as Cabinet Office minister) and Jeremy Heywood (as PPS to Gordon Brown). They were attended by every member of the No. 10 Policy Unit (responsible for shadowing different departments), all key Communications staff, and all the key civil servants in the PM's private office.

As the cast list suggests, behind the Cabinet meetings, these were the most important meetings of the week in Downing Street.

Upcoming announcements by other departments would be challenged, more information sought, and – because each item would get at least two airings before it was due to be announced – it was (to quote Hilton) 'inconceivable' that something would be announced without No. 10 knowing about it, let alone something that they didn't agree with.

Take a hypothetical example of how it would work: DEFRA submit an item for the grid one week which simply says they'll be consulting on options for the rationalisation and improved management of the state-owned forest estate, and they plan to announce this in ten days' time. A couple of curious people round the table say: 'What's this about?' and tell the DEFRA policy shadow to find out more information and get a copy of the consultation paper.

Next Friday, there's a lot more detail in the document about the proposal, which DEFRA now plan to announce in three days' time, at which point everyone around the table says: 'Hold on a minute, they want to privatise the forests?! Get it out of the grid, and set up a meeting ASAP for the PM and the Secretary of State to discuss it. But tell them under no circumstances is this going ahead next week, and if they've briefed any Sunday papers, they'd better un-brief it sharpish or we'll dump all over it.'

So my question is – if what Steve Hilton told his students at Stanford is true – what on earth has happened to the No. 10 grid system? It's clearly not working as it once did, as is occasionally obvious from the confusion over what's being announced and when, the clashes between different good announcements, and the waste of other good announcements on days when bad news is sure to dominate.

Losing the civil servant master of the grid, Paul Brown MBE – who retired early in the coalition – would have been a blow, but I'm sure his replacement(s) are just as thorough when it comes to making sure the Upcoming Business document is both exhaustive and digestible. My guess is that the apparent failure of the grid system is much less to do with the quality of the civil service legwork going into it, and more about the importance accorded it by the No. 10 political machine.

Here are two straws in the wind which may support that theory:

1. One of Craig Oliver's first acts as Director of Communications in No. 10 was to alter the structure of the grid so the week started on a Sunday not on a Monday. A tiny but significant change, because what it revealed was a mindset that the grid was just a news management tool, and news management for each week starts with what's in the Sunday papers and who's going on *Marr*. Whereas the old system – when the week started when Parliament was sitting – reflected a mindset that the grid was chiefly about controlling government business and announcements, not controlling the media; and

2. I was chatting before Christmas to two relatively young, junior members of Downing Street staff – very bright, pleasant, energetic types – and I asked them in passing: 'Who's chairing the grid meetings these days?' After all, based on past history, it

could be Craig Oliver, Francis Maude or Chris Martin (David Cameron's current PPS). Or based on seniority in today's No. 10, it could be Andrew Cooper, Ed Llewellyn or even George Osborne. One of them answered, 'I'm not sure.' The other answered, 'I don't know if we still do grid meetings.' Now, as I say, they were junior, but the idea that what used to be the second most important meeting of the week in Downing Street is now one that is barely on the radar of two members of No. 10 staff seems deeply worrying to me.

We're forever being told that David Cameron, George Osborne and their teams are devotees of Tony Blair's style of government, but if they have genuinely ditched or downgraded *the* key mechanism by which his Downing Street managed the business of government, it is a shocking blind spot in their devotion, and one that needs correcting. Sharpish.

WHY DID THE GRID WITHER?

14 JANUARY 2013

H AVING ARGUED YESTERDAY that the demise of the grid system explains a lot of the problems the government has been having, as well as the oddly stoical response of Steve Hilton, I'm going to consider today the possible rationale for that demise.

Let's remember that, in the early days of this government, it leaked like an old church roof. Michael Gove was almost destroyed by leaks in his first months at Education, and just ten days after the coalition was formed, we saw the unprecedented leaking of the entire Queen's Speech to the intrepid Sunday pairing of Paddy Hennessy and Vincent Moss.

The leaking of that period was mostly blamed on disgruntled, Labour-friendly civil servants, although – in my experience and the experience of most people with leaky roofs – the more drips there are, the heavier the flow gets and the more diverse the sources.

If you're a brand-new minister or special adviser, keen to build relationships with the media, nothing is more tempting than leaking the odd titbit that you've seen in a Cabinet paper, especially if you're in coalition and owe no party loyalty to the minister concerned, and if you know those ubiquitous 'Whitehall moles' are going to get the blame.

Now, in that context – if you're Steve Hilton or Andy Coulson in May 2010 – do you view the existence of an 'Upcoming Business' document detailing every government announcement for the next fortnight as a helpful tool for good government, or as a massive hole in your defence against leaks?

Do you regard the grid traditionally circulated across government (minus the accompanying detailed document) as a helpful device to ensure departments and ministers know the plan for each day, or as an invitation for untrustworthy colleagues to sit down over a pint with journalists and try to work out what 'Forest Management Consultation' might mean? (Erm, a posthumous knighthood for Brian Clough?)

And the reality is, for all its success as an organisational tool under New Labour, the grid and the 'Upcoming Business' document were the source of many a leak. A whole journalistic phrasebook exists because of it: 'busting the grid' or 'a bit of gridology', all code for using the headlines in the grid to decipher an upcoming announcement.

So an enterprising journalist might be told by a friendly adviser that there's an interesting line in the grid saying: 'Trains: Alcohol'. He or she does a bit of Googling to see what the IPPR, the BMA, the Police Federation or others have been recommending. They then call the Home Office late on a Friday and say:

> Hi, I've had a briefing about this trains and booze story for next week, which is all fine – we're probably going to splash it – and I've got all the quotes I need, but I'm a bit unclear which of your ministers is making the statement – is it the boss or one of the juniors? Ah, OK. And the only other thing I'm unclear about is will there be options in the document, or is it just the main proposal? Ah, OK. And what's the official way you'd like that worded so we don't set any hares running? Ah, fine. Let me get that down. Thanks very much.

Now of course it isn't always as easy as all that. But over the New Labour years, many a story was fleshed out and stood up from a couple of words in the grid, let alone the several paragraphs of detail found in the 'Upcoming Business' document.

So, going back to Hilton and Coulson, you can absolutely see why one of the first things they did on entering Downing Street – upon facing a string of damaging leaks – was to reduce the number of people allowed to attend the grid meetings, reduce the copy list for the 'Upcoming Business' document, and both restrict and delay the circulation of the grid across Whitehall.

Nevertheless, in an unsuccessful effort to solve one problem (the leaks continued anyway, witness Budget 2012), they created another, far bigger problem: losing the control that the grid offered them over the government machine, perhaps before they'd realised its importance in that respect.

I can imagine why Hilton stopped attending the grid meetings: not just because they were Coulson's show, but because once you haven't got all the right people round the table, they cease to be of any value.

Every government faces leaks; they're annoying, but they're rarely fatally damaging. What is fatal is the government losing grip over what it's announcing, how, when and, most importantly, why. If the price you pay for that grip is the occasional unscheduled Sunday-paper splash, it's worth every penny.

EXTREME LENTING 2013

12 FEBRUARY 2013

'TELL ME WHY', Neil Young sang, 'is it hard to make arrangements with yourself?'

Why do we find it so hard to give things up, even for a temporary period, and not just things to which we are chemically addicted, but even bad habits or over-indulgences?

This week, now that the amateurs behind 'Dry January' have concluded their warm-up act, the professionals will take the stage: millions of Catholics in Britain and Ireland attempting to give up one of their main pleasures for the 46-day duration of Lent.

Whether they will succeed or not depends in part on what psychological strategy they adopt when deciding what to give up.

Some, especially couples, will use the buddy system – giving up something together, and policing each other's adherence. Others will introduce an element of competition, betting a friend to see whose resolve can last longest.

For me, the best strategy is to ask someone who knows you well what they are certain you could not give up for forty-six days. Once they've got the abuse out of the way ('being a tosser' etc.), you usually get some on-the-money suggestions, from booze to swearing.

The desire to show a good friend that they don't know you as well as they think is a powerful motivator. And having surprised many of them last year by succeeding in giving up alcohol for the duration, I requested an even more stretching challenge this time round.

One friend suggested Arsenal, but I'm not sure that would be a sufficient hardship this season. Then another friend, watching me tuck into a chicken curry the other night, stated with total confidence that I could not give up meat for forty-six days.

Now there's a challenge.

I'm the guy who goes to J Sheekey or Livebait and orders the steak. When forced to attend a management away-day at the Jamyang Buddhist retreat centre in Kennington yesterday, I smuggled in a packet of ham to have with the 'lunch' provided. When Hitler's food-taster confirmed last week that he was a strict vegetarian, I nodded as though a great riddle had been solved. I like meat a lot.

So not only did I tell my friend I accepted the challenge and would give up eating the beasts of the field for forty-six days, but – like Houdini adding a few extra padlocks – I added the other staples of my diet, betting I could go without wheat and potatoes for the duration as well.

Pasta, pastry, bread, chips, crisps, mash and my beloved lager – all forsaken – along with chicken, beef, lamb, pork and whatever they're putting in the frozen lasagne this week.

Tonight will be my carnival (from the Latin 'carne vale' – farewell to meat), spaghettival and lagerval all in one – a last feast before the fast.

Usually at this stage, I'd be expected to point you towards my Just Giving page and ask for sponsorship, but – unlike Bob Geldof – I don't want your fockin' money.

If you care to support my efforts, I'd ask you to do something much more important: go and sign up to the 'Enough Food for Everyone … IF' campaign via CAFOD or, for all the heathens out there, via the IF website direct.

Because I haven't just chosen meat, wheat and 'tatoes because they're the staples of my diet, but because they're symbolic of the problems being highlighted by the IF campaign:

Meat because, in many countries in the developing world, land that would be used by small farmers to grow food for their communities is being seized from them to make way for the big agricultural corporations, who will use the land for export crops, for the manufacture of biofuels or for grazing livestock, all for the benefit of motorists and meat-eaters in more prosperous countries;

Wheat because, along with other seeds and grains, trade in them is increasingly controlled by a small number of massive multi-nationals, able to manipulate markets, if necessary by withholding stocks, and ensure that only those large-scale farmers in their supply chains are supplied with the seeds and grains that they need; and

Potatoes because, almost 170 years on from the famine that devastated Ireland, we are still seeing countries today which are exporting food even as their own people go hungry; countries like Zambia, with the third worst rate of hunger in the world, lauded by the World Bank for its openness to multinationals growing food for export while avoiding tax on their profits.

Shady land deals and tax evasion by multinationals; the squeezing-out of small farmers from fair access to land, credit, seeds and markets; and the misuse of land that should be growing food for local communities – these are some of the key root causes of hunger in the developing world that the IF campaign seeks to tackle, and is asking George Osborne and David Cameron to take action on in the March Budget and the June G8 summit.

My Lent fasting won't make any difference to those problems, but the hole I'll feel in my stomach each lunchtime at work will remind me why I'm there. If you'd like to play your part, please sign up.

OF SWIMMING, SUBSIDIES
AND CIVIL SERVANTS

25 FEBRUARY 2013

DOMINIC LAWSON'S EXCELLENT article in today's *Independent* asks why the state 'subsidy' which allows our major national museums and galleries to be open free of charge to the public is considered more important than the right to free swimming for children and pensioners scrapped by the coalition.

His article also repeats the complaint by the increasingly luminous Labour MP Tristram Hunt that the Potteries Museum and Art Gallery in his constituency and other regional collections face unfair competition from their no more impressive national counterparts because of the free admission subsidy enjoyed by the latter.

These are good points and an important debate, but it's worth looking back at the context of the Labour government's original decision to underwrite free admission to the national collections in 2001, when I was the Treasury civil servant responsible for – amongst other things – VAT policy.

At that time, those museums and galleries who had traditionally been free of charge – and their patrons – were putting huge pressure on the government about their VAT bills. Because they did not charge for admission, they were not conducting a business for VAT purposes, and could not therefore reclaim the VAT incurred in running their buildings: heating, upkeep etc.

They proposed various wheezes to get around their VAT bills, all totally illegal under UK or European VAT law, but ultimately they kept coming back to the obvious solution: charging for entry, and running themselves as businesses. And let's not kid ourselves, there were many finance directors of those museums and galleries who were quite happy to see that as the solution and take a fiver a head from the adult tourists pouring through their doors each year.

Tony Blair and then Culture Secretary Chris Smith were determined not to have that happen, and after a particularly difficult meeting at No. 10 with the great arts patron Sir Dennis Mahon (still fighting the same battles from beyond the grave, according to Dominic Lawson's article), the terse instruction came through by email from D. Miliband (then a No. 10 Spad) to E. Miliband (then a No. 11 Spad): 'Get this sorted.'

It wasn't often Brown's Treasury was given orders on tax policy by Blair's Downing Street, but this was one such occasion. So after discussing it with Paymaster General Dawn Primarolo, Ed Miliband called me in, and – despite me telling him and Dawn the sixteen different reasons we couldn't legally do what Dennis Mahon and co. were proposing – Ed kept smiling out of one corner of his mouth, and said: 'You've got to find a way ... We need you to find a way.'

The trouble was that trying to force a solution in this area was hugely risky at a time when Brussels VAT Commissioner Herr Fritz Bolkenstein was itching for an excuse to open a wide-ranging inquiry into all the ways in which the UK VAT system 'illegally' diverged from EC VAT rules, particularly where new 'reliefs' had been introduced that were not protected by the UK's original accession treaties from back when we introduced VAT in 1973.

The perennial fear was that an inquiry into one new VAT relief could easily spill into the European Court of Justice examining all the other ones we'd introduced or extended over the years since 1973 and, for example, ruling illegal our (extended) VAT zero rates for children's clothes and shoes. So when I sat down with two brilliant Customs and Excise civil servants, David Ogilvie and Judith Warner, it wasn't far off trying to defuse a bomb inside an ammunition dump.

However, without going into all the dull intricacies of the special provisions of Sections 33 and 34 of the VAT Act 1994,[16] which allow

---

16 Over the last two years, I've read about No. 10's plans to devolve responsibility to local authorities to discharge certain services and open up competition with private providers at local level, and we've recently heard that George Osborne is examining similar proposals from Michael Heseltine for the Budget. Whenever I've read those reports, I've thought: 'Hmm, I hope someone's thought about the implications of that for Section 33', which is the provision that allows local authorities to claim VAT refunds on their spending under certain, very prescribed circumstances. If they haven't and they're about to mess around with those arrangements, I'd suggest an urgent word with David Ogilvie and Judith Warner, wherever they are these days.

for VAT rebate schemes for certain ring-fenced groups of bodies providing certain qualifying non-business services as a result of the funding they receive from central government (believe me, you don't want me to), we were able to find a convoluted way of refunding a prescribed group of museums and galleries their VAT bills.

That's why when the 'Section 33A Refund Scheme for National Museums and Galleries' was announced in 2001, it was tightly ring-fenced to those bodies who were in receipt of DCMS funding due to the status of their collections – hence it could not be extended to the Potteries Museum and Art Gallery, but equally it could not be legally challenged by Herr Bolkenstein or by the French or Italian tourist industries.

So I hope that answers Tristram Hunt's question (albeit not in a way that will satisfy him). It does not answer Dominic Lawson's point about why free tours round the Tate are considered worthier of subsidy than free swimming for pensioners, but I hope it explains the background to the current arrangements.

And ahead of my appearance at the Public Administration Select Committee tomorrow morning, who have called me to come and answer questions about 'The Future of the Civil Service', it's a useful illustration that – nine times out of ten – when civil servants are told: 'We want this done', they will do their best to find a way.

GOING TO THE MATTRESSES:
THE ART OF SURVIVING A COUP

10 MARCH 2013

YET AGAIN, THE Sunday papers are full of speculation about the threats to David Cameron's leadership, revolving this time around what we might charitably call yesterday's 'wide-ranging' speech by the Home Secretary about what it will take to win the next election.

This stuff will rumble on interminably unless Plan A eventually comes up trumps – no other issue will matter in the meantime – or until some Massive External Event comes along that gives David Cameron the chance to show that he is still the only person for the job.

My advice to No. 10 is that neither of those scenarios is worth worrying about – i.e. don't for goodness' sake start drafting speeches in response to hypothetical Massive External Events (not on email anyway), and if they're determined to stick to Plan A, there's nothing to do but see what happens.

What I think they should be spending their time planning for is what happens if all the speculation, rumbling and agitation comes to a sudden head; if someone somewhere decides to force the issue.

For me, all the talk of stalking horses and leadership contests is an anachronistic nonsense. Not since Margaret Thatcher twenty-three years ago has a party leader had to resign following a formal leadership challenge.

Since then, four have been compelled to resign (or pre-resign in Tony Blair's case) as a result of pressure from within their own party, and five as a result of general election defeat. Only Paddy Ashdown and, in tragic circumstances, John Smith escaped either fate.

Britain's modern party leaders are not ousted by stalking horses; they are dragged from their beds in the dead of night, and shot in the courtyard with a Sky News helicopter overhead. So it would be extremely foolish for anyone in No. 10 to take the complex rules required to mount a leadership challenge as a reason to relax.

No, when it comes, if it ever comes, I'd guess the attempted ousting of the PM will look like this, all familiar features of past coups:

- Leading Cabinet plotters will deliver subtle but incendiary speeches, interviews or articles, calling for a change of approach or style;

- Joint letters will be submitted to No. 10 by symbolically important groups of MPs, including heavyweight ex-Cabinet ministers;

- With sorrowful and suitably devastating statements, some junior ministers and PPSs will resign, saying they no longer feel able to serve;

- One or more major donors to the party will withdraw their support; and

- Above all, supposedly loyal or senior members of the Cabinet will become suddenly absent and turn deadly silent.

These moves will not be the starting gun for a leadership challenge; they will be the sniper rifles attempting to finish the job there and then, by generating enough party pressure and media frenzy that the PM's resignation becomes inevitable.

So what No. 10 should be asking themselves is: how well prepared are we if and when that day comes? And if they want to know what it takes to get through an attempted coup, they could do worse than study the record of Gordon Brown – the Charles de Gaulle of Downing Street when it came to surviving assassination attempts. Based on the Brown survival manual, I would ask them the following five key questions:

1. **How far in advance do you know what's coming?**

Gordon Brown had hands-down the best intelligence operation of any recent PM. We were having conference calls and going through the 'secret' lists and plans of rebels signed up to the September 2008 Blairite plot a full fortnight before they moved into action. By contrast, Brown's operation knew the Geoff Hoon and Patricia Hewitt coup in January 2010 was a shambolic effort with no support precisely because they didn't know about it in advance. And I say that with no pleasure given I'm a big fan of Geoff's, and one of Patricia's former officials. But that level of intelligence-gathering doesn't happen by accident: it's about cultivating moles; taking talkative, sociable types out for drinks; testing the water with individuals by privately venting (and exaggerating) your own concerns about the future; and above all, keeping your eyes and ears open for unusual couplings or hushed conversations. But that all required hard work and ceaseless vigilance, so what I'd ask No. 10 is: who is currently putting in that effort for you?

2. **Who are your wartime consiglieres?**

Of course, good intelligence is only of value if you know what to do with it. Once you know what's happening, when, and who's involved, your No. 1 goal in defeating a coup is to make the whole thing look shambolic and doomed to fail, thereby shaping the media coverage and putting others off from joining.

Sometimes, the plotters do that job for you. Other times, where you know their plans in advance, your task is sabotage. So if X is waiting until Y resigns, and A, B and C are due to follow X, all your effort goes into delaying or preventing the resignation of Y, at which point – when the expected announcement doesn't pop up on News 24 – the others get cold feet, and Z – who was the first to resign – is left high and dry, as happened to James Purnell in 2009.

With David Miliband's various abortive coups, there was a certain crude art to inducing their failure. I was often personally criticised for over-reacting to some new Miliband manoeuvre, 'ramping it up' as people would say. But given David's tendency to treat rebellion like a reluctant bather inching his way into the sea at Skegness, it made sense to push him right in at the outset, on the grounds that he'd run straight back to his towel and not try again for at least six months.

But all this requires a gift for battle planning, an eye for the enemy's weak spot and the ability to exploit the chaos you create. And what you need most of all when fending off a coup is the ability to flood the battlefield – in this case the Commons tea rooms and Millbank TV studios – with loyal soldiers prepared to work flat-out and take some bullets to ensure that the main noise in the ears of wavering MPs is unstinting support for the leader and criticism of the plotters.

3. **Do you know where each member of the Cabinet is, in all senses?**

The moment of maximum danger in an attempted coup is when Kay Burley says: 'We are yet to hear from the Home Secretary', or Nick Robinson says: 'The most intriguing thing I've heard, not confirmed yet, is that the Education Secretary – one of the PM's closest allies – did not try to persuade his PPS to stay on.' Once the test of a coup's momentum becomes the response of key Cabinet ministers, every hour of silence that ticks by piles pressure on the PM. So you need to know in advance where each individual is, and have a guaranteed way of getting a message through. If the response is they're in a meeting, then forget it – they're Fredo Corleone. If they answer, you tell them to get a statement on PA ASAP, and refusal is not an option, as was the case with Alistair Darling during the Hoon/Hewitt coup. You must put the questions in the mind of a wavering minister: How can I say no? And what if I get this wrong?

But right now, No. 10 need also to ask themselves about each Cabinet member: where is their head at? If they seem suddenly to be lunching more journalists, doing more speeches, appearing at more receptions, chatting more in the margins of Cabinet and doing less nodding when the PM talks, then they're probably already thinking about the next reshuffle after this PM has gone, or – in some cases – of taking his place. So, the question for No. 10 is: are you monitoring all of that, especially with those the PM considers his closest allies?

4. **How's your relationship with the media these days?**
As I've said, momentum is everything in an attempted coup: to succeed, the plotters must keep pushing the leader towards the cliff. The media are crucial in determining that momentum: if

they say it's fizzled out, then it has; if they say one more bad day will make the leader's position untenable, then it will.

But, even for the BBC, this is not an objective, scientific process; it's about 100 or so very influential people at different media outlets forming a view based on their conversations with each other and with key players on either side of the plot, as well as, to some extent, on public attitudes. That is why, no matter how bad the coverage of Gordon Brown's premiership became, it was still vital for us to maintain strong and friendly relationships with those 100 or so people.

So, when and if the day comes, the question is: do the PM, his genuine supporters, and his Communications advisers have strong enough relationships with the media that their reading of the situation will trump that of the rebels, or at least be given equal weight? If Craig Oliver and Liam Fox gave entirely opposite views to a senior political editor about whether an ongoing coup was likely to succeed, who would they currently be more inclined to trust?

5. **What are you prepared to concede to survive?**
    Perhaps the hardest question of all is if, despite all your efforts, you are still pushed towards the crisis point – where the media have decided one more bad day, resignation or letter will kill you – how do you save yourself? The only answer is to negotiate, perhaps not with the plotters directly, but with influential Cabinet ministers or party figures, asking them what it will take to reach a deal.

So it's vital for the PM to ask himself how far he'd go to make the peace. Would he agree to replace individual advisers, change his style of government or cancel planned reshuffle moves, all compromises that Gordon Brown made to defuse different coups? Would he agree to move his Chancellor or bring forward an in/out referendum, having previously vowed to do neither? These are not decisions that should be made under the intense pressure of an attempted coup, but thought through rationally in advance, so that the twin temptations to concede too much, or to resign impetuously on principle, are both avoided.

My final reflection on Gordon Brown's record of overcoming coups, is that – however arduous or brutal some of the methods were – his instinct for survival was there for a reason, in that (by the time the global financial crisis started) he knew why he wanted to be in No. 10 and what he wanted to achieve – even if he often struggled to explain it.

If that instinct for survival – and everything that goes with it – is lacking in No. 10 at present, then it may point to a wider problem; with apologies to John Rentoul's Banned List, something of an existential crisis. Which makes the timing of Theresa May's speech all the more damaging, given that she showed with some level of detail and verve why she'd like to be in No. 10 and what she'd want to achieve.

And yet, there is so much for the current incumbents in Downing Street to live for, so many reasons to do what it takes to survive.

After all, you never know when the next Massive External Event will come along. And perhaps Plan A will eventually come up trumps. Stranger things have happened.

THE BUDGET AND THE
BLOKE IN THE PUB

19 MARCH 2013

TWO IMMEDIATE THOUGHTS on Ben Brogan's superbly insightful and well-informed piece about Wednesday's upcoming Budget and the Lynton Crosby impact on Tory messaging.

1. First, the latter. It sounds eminently sensible on paper for the government to talk solely about the issues that are the public's priorities for the two years until the election. But how do you decide what their priorities are?

According to Ben, the answer from the PM's pollster Andrew Cooper is by asking people: 'What issue would you raise with the PM in the pub if he came in for a pint?', to which the overwhelming answer seems to be 'immigration'.

The trouble with all that is that, frankly, there's a certain kind of person who bangs on about politics in the pub, and you don't necessarily want to base your political strategy around them.

I'd say in general that what wins elections is targeting the kind of voters whose first question if the current PM walked into their pub would be: 'Alright fella, what's the Queen like?', or 'Do you think Villa are going to stay up?', or even just 'How are you, mate?', rather than 'What are you going to do about those Romanians?'

It does all slightly remind me of Tony Blair's obsession – encouraged by Philip Gould – with talking about anti-social behaviour, then law 'n' order more widely, and eventually the catch-all theme of 'security' in the run-up to the 2005 election, because these were the issues that people would 'raise in the pub'.

What Tony found is that the more he banged on about anti-social behaviour, the more the media and the public identified it as a big issue, and the harder it became to demonstrate that the government was capable of doing anything about it commensurate to the scale of the 'problem' he himself had talked up. So it played into then Tory leader Michael Howard's hands.

Of course, this made Gordon Brown tear his hair out. He argued – correctly – that Labour would win the 2005 election, as it had done in 1997 and 2001, by focusing on the economy, jobs and public services, and the more the government itself talked up another issue as the main public priority, the harder it would be to get back to that core agenda.

So – in light of that – tempting though it might be for the Tories just to talk about those 'pub issues' of immigration and welfare for the next two years – I reckon they'd be handing a bit of an open goal to Labour if that's at the expense of talking about the economy, the NHS, police and schools.

2. On the first point, if Ben's correct that George Osborne is going for a 'steady as she goes' Budget, similar to that called for by Ed Staite, then there's a certain logic to that, i.e. if there's no money for any fireworks, and he doesn't want any scope for pasty-style disasters, then he should keep it simple.

Gordon Brown often did Budgets and PBRs like that, with very few 'big-ticket' measures, usually in the fallow years in the middle of the Parliament.

But in those years, Gordon did something else that George could learn from: when the gruel was thin, he always poured in a few small dollops of honey so there were some positive stories on the day, and some ways of demonstrating that he was conscious of the pressures on working people, not least for the backbenchers who had to hit the doorsteps that weekend.

Look through Gordon's Budgets and you will see a pattern of small but populist measures sprinkled through every one aimed at core lower- and middle-income households, from freezes in beer duty to reduced rates of VAT on everything from children's car seats to tampons. Never enough to affect the bottom line; never a headline measure; but enough to affect public perceptions.

I remember telling Gordon that, before I'd started working as his Head of Communications – on one of my spells back in Customs – I'd watched the 2003 Budget in a backstreet boozer in Southwark. As I watched the TV, I had one eye on a bloke who stood at the fruit machine underneath.

He looked up at the TV screen just three times in the entire Budget: once when Gordon said fags were going up 8p a packet ('Fuck's sake', he said); once when he said spirits duty would be frozen ('Wayyy!'); and once when he said he was abolishing bingo duty ('Waheeeey!!!' he said, turning to the barman, 'My mum's going to go nuts').

He then called his mum and told her about it, including the immortal phrase 'You won't be calling Gordon Brown a wanker again, will ya?'

I tell that story for a simple reason. That bingo measure cost £20 million – about the same as would have been raised from the pasty tax.

George Osborne would be forgiven this year for not wanting to see a single submission from the tax officials who delivered him VAT on pasties and the granny tax last time round.

But instead he should have told them:

> Right you lot, we screwed up last time cos I asked you to raise £2 billion in a painless way, and I didn't check the proposals out thoroughly enough. This time, I want the opposite of pasties:

the small stuff I can do that will set the tone of the Budget without costing us too much.

I can tell you, tax officials love that kind of Budget even more than the revenue-raising kind. I always did. And if George thinks Gordon has already picked off all the low-hanging fruit, I'd only recommend he should go back to the tree and see if it's growing again, for example:

- Gordon abolished TV licences for pensioners; George could abolish the surcharge for poorer households who pay by direct debit;

- Gordon expanded the sizes of clothes and shoes that qualified for the children's zero rate; George could do so again (it's twelve years since Gordon made his change – kids have grown since then); and

- As Robert Halfon MP has observed, there's an easy change that (I believe) can still be made to the specification of Ultra Low Sulphur Diesel to bring pump prices down, without costing a penny (except through VAT).

In short, if George Osborne tells his backbenchers that there's no scope for tax cuts, well – fair enough – but let's hope he's looked at all the options, not just the big ones called for by the Opposition and his own backbenchers.

I agree with Ben Brogan and Ed Staite that the Chancellor should keep things simple, and I think he should aim to deliver the shortest Budget in history (forty-four minutes would do it), but he shouldn't do that at the expense of a few small, symbolic measures to show he 'gets it'.

George, Andrew Cooper and Lynton Crosby need to ask themselves: what will that bloke under the telly in the pub in Southwark be ringing his mum about after this budget? It may not be granny taxes or pasties this time, but if he just keeps playing the fruit machine and never looks up at the screen, that's probably your worst outcome of all.

As if thinking about 'the bloke in the pub', the headline measure in George Osborne's 2013 Budget turned out to be a 1 pence cut in the duty on beer. In his 2014 Budget, he cut a further penny off beer duty and halved the tax paid on bingo company profits.

STANDARD PRACTICE

19 MARCH 2013

The 2013 Budget was marked by controversy after an online edition of the Standard *newspaper appeared with full details of the Budget measures and fiscal arithmetic before the Chancellor had even started his speech.*

A QUICK COMMENT ON the *Standard* controversy, just because a few people have asked me what the practice was under Gordon Brown.

Obviously, the *Standard* are in a hideous position on Budget Day, especially lunchtime Budgets, with an edition usually going off stone while the Chancellor's on his feet, but hitting the streets after he's sat down, in which they're required to have maybe three to four pages of coverage and a splash.

So the way it usually works is this: you have a strictly confidential discussion with the *Evening Standard* political editor on the morning of the Budget or the night before, which just ensures they know broadly what they'll be writing about later and can plan their pages accordingly.

The tone of that initial conversation is things like: 'Big push on housing'; 'Small boost for pensioners'; 'New efficiency measures on public spending'; 'Tough message on public sector pay'; 'Massive tax avoidance crackdown – that's the biggest new money coming in'; 'Little bit of a surprise on beer duty'; and 'Big measure at the end on job creation – that's the biggest money going out'.

Incidentally, you have exactly the same discussion with the broadcasters on the morning of the Budget given they have to react in real-time and prepare packages for the news bulletins afterwards.

That conversation is also a chance for the *Standard* to ask how reliable the stories are that have appeared in other newspapers in the previous week, to which your responses might vary from: 'I think that's pretty safe' or 'I'd steer clear of that one' to 'They're in the right territory but the figures are wrong'.

Again, that helps them plan their pages, and – where you've indicated a story is safe – they can write it pretty hard to save themselves a job later.

There is then a second crucial conversation with the *Standard*, which I always had only after Gordon had stood up to speak in the House – and usually in a frantic two-minute whisper outside the parliamentary press gallery – where I'd go through all the themes I'd referred to earlier and fill in the gaps with detailed facts and numbers.

The political editor would then run off and make the necessary additions to his stories, fire them off to the *Standard* news desk and the presses would begin to roll. While doing so, he'd also keep one ear on the Budget as it was being announced in case I'd left anything of interest out, but frankly I never did.

So, in short, the *Standard* would have no detailed facts or figures on individual measures or taxes until Gordon had stood up, and there was no risk of any of those figures hitting the streets before Gordon had sat down. It was a tried and tested process that almost never went wrong, although I'll admit it might have been a bit more difficult in the days of Twitter.[17]

Now, importantly, I can never remember in any of those conversations I had over the years giving any indications or hints on growth or borrowing or any of the key market-sensitive fiscal figures. That's partly because, in the days I was doing the job, that was rarely where the attention was focused, which is clearly a bit different today.

---

17 We did have one cock-up, which I still remember with a shudder, especially after today's events. I think it was an afternoon rather than a lunchtime Budget, so the *Standard* had already done one edition based on a very broad initial conversation saying things like: 'The Chancellor is set to give a boost to pensioners' and 'Gordon Brown is expected to ease the burden on motorists'. In their rush to get the next edition printed after Gordon had stood up, the *Standard* inserted the details into those sentences, but didn't change the tense of them – so it read as though they were still speculating but with the exact detail of what he was going to announce. The paper didn't hit the streets until after Gordon had sat down, but questions were still asked in the House about it.

But it's also the fact that – whether it was the Budget numbers twice a year or ONS data every month – I knew it was career death for me (and possibly Gordon) to take any risk on market-sensitive numbers leaking in advance.[18]

So, what did I make of today's events? Well, clearly, it was an unfortunate cock-up at the *Standard*'s end, and I'm sure they're mortified about landing the very helpful Treasury officials and advisers in trouble.

But I wouldn't say those officials and advisers are entirely innocent. It seems to me: 1) they must have had the second, detailed conversation too early, or possibly given out too much detail in the initial conversation; and 2) they also divulged stuff in advance which frankly they never should because of its market-sensitivity.

As for the *Standard* themselves, if the Treasury choose to divulge that level of information and do so too early in the day, what are they meant to say? 'Hold on, I think you're telling me too much too soon'? Of course not.

And it's the telling of too much too soon that's caused the problem – not the long-standing arrangements that I've described, or even the *Standard*'s cock-up in posting their splash online – so I hope no one in the Treasury will think about abandoning those arrangements as a consequence, and I hope no one at the *Standard* is in any trouble tonight.

---

18 There was one occasion when Gordon was adamant for at least two hours on the night of a Budget that he was going to have to resign – after he personally had inadvertently leaked every single market-sensitive number in the forecast. But, with apologies for being a tease, I'll save that cracking story for another day...

2010: A PARTICULARLY
SHARP INTAKE

26 MARCH 2013

THIS FEELS LIKE déjà-vu, but I had a quick thought on Ben Brogan's latest essential article on the mood inside the Tory Party, especially his conclusion that its next leader may come from the hugely ambitious and variously talented group of MPs first elected in 2010.

There are many Labour types who look at the superb calibre of its own 2010 intake, and think the same thing. Well, what are their chances?

The whole idea of the 'intake' may not mean anything to anyone outside Westminster, but it matters hugely inside. For MPs, it's equivalent to your year-group at school or university, but even more so, since they tend always to be four to five years apart from the intake on either side.

Just like at school, it throws up rivalries and tensions, but equally a sense of solidarity, and certainly a desire that your group should be regarded as the lead candidates for promotion and advancement, provided of course that you are one of those advanced.

It was hugely symbolic that, in 2006, members of every recent intake wrote to Tony Blair calling for him to set out plans for a stable and orderly succession to Gordon Brown; it showed – in a way nothing else could have done – that there was broad (although not universal) support for that view amongst the younger Labour backbenchers.

So what does history tell us about the chances of the Class of 2010? Well, if we assume that modern British politics began in 1975 with the selection of Margaret Thatcher as Tory leader, then this has been the sequence of Tory leaders, alongside the year they first entered the House of Commons and how long they led the party for:

> Thatcher: 1959 – leads from 1975–90 (fifteen years)
>
> Major: 1979 – leads from 1990–97 (seven years)
>
> Hague/IDS/Howard: 1989/1992/1983 – collectively lead from 1997–2005 (eight years)
>
> Cameron: 2001 – leads from 2005 to present (seven years and counting)

Now, I'm cheating a little by bracketing together the group of Tory leaders who took on Tony Blair as PM, but – strategically

– that was a weird period in Tory history, and I'll long argue that the Tories should have stuck with William Hague even after 2001, and that the short reigns of IDS and Howard were an aberration.

As our internal polls used to tell us, there were a number of Tory leaders who could potentially have beaten Tony Blair in 2005, and Hague was arguably one of them. Michael Howard definitely wasn't.

Anyway, if we imagine – not implausibly – that Hague had seen the Tories through two elections, then we'd observe a pattern where – for every seven to eight years a Tory leader is in charge – recent history suggests that the intake from which their successor is drawn shifts forward around ten years.

Which would mean – if the Tories decide to unseat David Cameron in the coming year or more likely, as Ben says, after the next election – then it is indeed most likely his successor would come from the 2010 intake, even though none of the current Cabinet come from that group.

Of course, the optimistic scenario for Cameron loyalists is that he wins the next election and the one after that, and steps down in 2020 after matching Lady Thatcher, and leading the party for fifteen years. In which case, the pattern would suggest his successor would come from that 2020 intake. Boris, anyone?

And what of Labour, which has been quicker to advance members of the 2010 intake to its front bench, notably Chuka Umunna and Rachel Reeves? Their recent history – since the Thatcher period began – is even clearer. Look at the list of intakes from which their last seven leaders have been drawn:

Jim Callaghan: 1945

Michael Foot: 1945

Neil Kinnock: 1970

John Smith: 1970

Tony Blair: 1983

Gordon Brown: 1983

Ed Miliband: 2005[19]

So the pattern is that – while their periods in office differ – the Labour leadership tends to skip several intakes at a time, and shifts forward around twelve to fifteen years each pair of leaders that go by. That would suggest the next Labour leader will – like Ed Miliband – come from the 2005 intake, but the one after that is not yet in Parliament, and will take his or her seat for the first time in the 2020 election.

Of course, patterns are made to be broken, and all this may change. But, right now and mainly because I'm a great believer in political history repeating itself, I'd have my money on Cameron's successor coming from the 2010 Tory intake, but their exceptional Labour equivalents – Chuka, Rachel, Tristram Hunt, Gloria De Piero, Michael Dugher, Jonathan Ashworth and many more

---

19 Of course, it's also worth noting from the sequences above that – the Howard aberration aside – neither main party in the modern era has gone back to a previous intake to select its new leader. There are good explanations for that on both sides, but nevertheless, if you were placing your bets the way you always must in the Grand National – taking past history into account – you wouldn't see why William Hague, Theresa May, David Miliband and Yvette Cooper are the bookies' favourites to take the lead if Ed or Dave fall at Becher's, given that they are all from previous intakes.

– having to settle for great Cabinet careers instead of the top job.

So the question for them becomes not which one of us is ahead of the others, but which one of us is capable of breaking the mould?

THE PROMISED LAND

3 APRIL 2013

THIS NIGHT FORTY-FIVE years ago, Martin Luther King came off his sickbed to the Mason Temple in Memphis, Tennessee, where a large crowd had gathered for a campaign rally in support of striking sanitation workers.

Memphis encapsulated the problem that the civil rights movement faced after 1965, once its focus switched from civil rights and voting rights in Southern states to the problems of black poverty, police abuse and economic discrimination in the major American cities:

How do you make a strike by sanitation workers for better wages and working conditions the same kind of moral issue as blacks in the South being denied the vote or forced to use segregated facilities?

How do you put pressure on faceless corporations through marches and boycotts when you do not face the same open police brutality and white violence that shocked the world when the same tactics were used in the South?

And how do you retain the support of white liberals and the White House itself when your protest is wrapped up with rioting and the activities of the Black Power movement, as it was in Memphis?

Martin Luther King tried to address these challenges in his 'Promised Land' speech on 3 April 1968, which I believe – partly because of the circumstances and the timing, but mainly because of the scintillating argument and soaring rhetoric – is the greatest speech ever made. It's worth reading in full, but these are for me the highest points:

WHICH AGE WOULD YOU LIKE TO LIVE IN?

A magnificent opening theme, where MLK imagines the Almighty inviting him to choose an age to live in, allowing him to conduct a rapid survey of history from Moses through to Memphis, and proclaim that now is a more important time than ever:

> I can remember, I can remember when Negroes were just going around as Ralph has said, so often, scratching where they didn't itch, and laughing when they were not tickled. But that day is

all over. We mean business now, and we are determined to gain our rightful place in God's world.

TELL THEM NOT TO BUY HART'S BREAD

How many great speeches in history contain detailed instructions for direct action campaigning, including which banks, breadmakers and milk companies to boycott? Yet here, MLK makes a practical reality of his rhetoric on forcing change, and persuades his audience of their collective power.

THE ROAD TO JERICHO

MLK's retelling of the parable of the Good Samaritan is brilliant in his personalisation of the story and his almost comic empathy with the priest and the Levite who passed by the stricken man, arguing that they asked themselves: 'If I stop to help this man, what will happen to me?' But then the Good Samaritan came by. And he reversed the question: 'If I do not stop to help this man, what will happen to him?'

WHILE IT SHOULD NOT MATTER

The reading of letters is a familiar rhetorical tool, used to great effect most recently by President Obama, but never used to greater effect here, than when MLK says he'd forgotten all the letters he received from the great and good when he was stabbed in New

York ten years previously, except one from a little girl, which he would never forget:

It said simply, 'Dear Dr King: I am a ninth-grade student at the White Plains High School.' She said, 'While it should not matter, I would like to mention that I am a white girl. I read in the paper of your misfortune, and of your suffering. And I read that if you had sneezed, you would have died. And I'm simply writing you to say that I'm so happy that you didn't sneeze.'

I'M GLAD I DIDN'T SNEEEEEEZE

Surely the strangest peroration in the history of great speeches, but it works astonishingly well, not least because of the aural reminders of the 'I Have a Dream' speech, and his inspiring tour of the great achievements of the civil rights movement. The crowd starts to build into a frenzy as he says: 'If I had sneezed, I wouldn't have been around in 1962, when Negroes in Albany, Georgia, decided to straighten their backs up. And whenever men and women straighten their backs up, they are going somewhere, because a man can't ride your back unless it is bent.'

THE MOUNTAINTOP

With the crowd clapping and cheering, MLK then drops his voice and his pace to tell of the threats on his life, and how it doesn't matter to him now. It's a sombre moment, instantly lifted as he explains in soaring tones why it doesn't matter:

> I just want to do God's will. And He's allowed me to go up to the mountain. And I've looked over. And I've seen the Promised Land. I may not get there with you. But I want you to know tonight, that we, as a people, will get to the Promised Land. And I'm happy, tonight. I'm not worried about anything. I'm not fearing any man. Mine eyes have seen the glory of the coming of the Lord.

In 1993, when history undergraduates at Cambridge were listening to pitches by the various faculty members for what they should choose as specialist subjects for their finals, Professor Tony Badger – who taught the civil rights movement course – played an audio recording of the last few minutes of the 'Promised Land' speech, switched the cassette player off, and then simply said:

'And the next day they shot him … If you want to sign up for the course, there's a sheet at the front.'

I think every one of us in the room did.

The day they shot him – 4 April 1968 – there were riots in most major American cities and university campuses with large black populations. Except Indianapolis. That was in no small part due to what I would regard as the greatest improvised speech of all time, Robert F. Kennedy's announcement of MLK's death to a campaign rally in the city:

> What we need in the United States is not division; what we need in the United States is not hatred; what we need in the United States is not violence and lawlessness, but is love, and wisdom,

and compassion toward one another, and a feeling of justice toward those who still suffer within our country, whether they be white or whether they be black.

And two months later they shot him too.

*　*　*

DEAR AMERICA: LETTERS HOME FROM VIETNAM

There's another anniversary today, which closely relates to the same time period. Twenty-five years ago today, the documentary film *Dear America: Letters Home from Vietnam* was first telecast by HBO in the United States, having premiered in film festivals the previous year.

It is to my mind the greatest documentary of all time, and with a beautifully simple concept: over documentary footage of the war and excerpts from news broadcasts, a montage of letters from soldiers who served in Vietnam is read out by some of the leading actors and actresses of the 1980s, all against the greatest soundtrack you'll ever hear, from the Beach Boys at the start of the war to Bruce Springsteen at the unveiling of the Vietnam War Memorial in Washington, DC.

Some will say the weakness of the film is that it doesn't convey anything of the war from the Vietnamese perspective, but that's not what the film is about: it's simply about the authentic experience of the war from the US soldiers who served there. Their letters are alternately revealing and heartbreaking, and you can get a sample of the film in clips or watch the whole thing on YouTube. I can't find it on a Region 2 DVD, but it's the main reason I keep my old VHS player in working operation.

FOURTEEN DAYS IN MAY, TWENTY-SIX YEARS AGO

20 MAY 2013

OVERNIGHT ON THE 20/21 May 1987, a 26-year-old Mississippian named Edward Earl Johnson was executed in the gas chamber, convicted of murdering a police officer when caught in the act of sexually assaulting a pensioner. There was no medical evidence against him, and he claimed that his 'confession' was extracted by police at gunpoint.

His final days in jail were captured in a BBC documentary called *Fourteen Days in May*. It was shown in November that year, and at a time when there were still annual debates and regular free votes in Parliament on the restoration of the death penalty, it had a profound impact on that debate, showing how easily a man could be executed despite serious doubts about his conviction.

On a human level, it is an intensely painful film to watch: an intelligent young man experiencing his own fate right to the end in a state of bewilderment; and his family, trusting to God and the justice system to see the right thing done, all the while preparing for Edward's death. You will never listen to the love song 'Always', by Atlantic Starr, the same way again, having heard it sung to a young man by his family, knowing it is the last time they will see him alive.

Recalling the anniversary of the execution last night, I stumbled across the transcripts of two interviews conducted with Don Cabana, Edward's prison warden, and Clive Stafford Smith, the British lawyer who fought to have him cleared, both of whom played prominent roles in the BBC film.

I'd recommend reading all the transcripts on the website, but below are extracts from the Cabana and Stafford Smith interviews, which I think should be read by anyone who casually calls for capital punishment to be brought back in Britain.

DON CABANA

In Evans's case his mother and father, he came from a really good family and, you know, the hardest thing was to have to tell a mother that it was time to say a final goodbye to her son. And when I told her that Sunday before the execution that it was time, she came over and she rested her hand on my arm and she said, 'I've known you now for six years and I know you're a good person and I know you have children of your own, please don't … don't kill my child.'

And, that's … that's … that's difficult.

Wardens also, I think, deep down inside they secretly hope for absolution from the inmate. And that's important because I think, at least my experience, was that every time I executed somebody it was like a little bit of me was dying along with them. And had any of the inmates that I knew well and had gotten close to and executed, failed to give me absolution it would have left me with a very empty, empty feeling.

In the case of Edward Earl Johnson, because he insisted on his innocence and prison officials are used to hearing that all the time. But where a death row prisoner's concerned, once they know they're gonna be executed, you know, invariably what happens is, I mean, they're not gonna jump up and say, 'Well, Hallelujah I might as well 'fess up, tell the truth, I did it.'

They will say that in their way, you know, if they say, 'Warden, would you apologise to the victim's family for me,' well hell, if you didn't do it then there's nothing to apologise for. Or 'Tell my momma I'm sorry.' You know, um, but in Edward's case, when I asked him if he had any final words, you know, his statement was, 'I'm innocent. I haven't been able to make anybody listen to me or believe me, and Warden, you know, in a few minutes you're about to become a murderer.'

Well, you know, there's a certain amount of role-play that goes on too and inmates and prison staff alike sometimes think they're supposed to play these macho roles to the very end, you know.

And, because I knew this kid and his grandmother who raised him, and I knew that he came from a religious family and in the prison he was very observant, he was, he didn't wear it on his sleeve for everybody to see. And so, I thought, you know, what if what we have here is the bravado thing to the very end.

And so I leaned down and whispered to him, I said:

'Son, I'm gonna step on out of the chamber here in a few minutes and as soon as that red phone rings, we're gonna have to proceed.'

And I said:

'You know what, there's twenty-something people standing around here, witnesses and staff and stuff, it's not important for any of them to hear you say – "I did it", OK. That doesn't matter.

'But what is important is that whatever the truth is, that, before I have to give the order, you have made peace between you and your God about the truth. He needs to hear you say what the truth is. Nobody else here needs to and they're not entitled to. You don't owe anybody here anything. But you owe yourself and you owe the God that you profess to believe in that clear understanding.'

And I thought, you know, this is pretty good stuff I'm saying here if he's just playing a role and he really did the crime and stuff, maybe this'll bring him around because I think you really think about … I said to the governor one time, 'Look, part of what Christianity preaches is redemption.' And I said, 'What if some prisoner that I execute might have achieved redemption next week, next month or next year? Once we've executed them that possibility's gone forever.'

And so that was important to me for this kid and he looked at me very calmly and he said, 'Warden, I'm at peace with my God, how are you gonna be with yours?' And, I walked out of that chamber convinced that he was innocent, I really did.

* * *

CLIVE STAFFORD SMITH

It was 21 May 1987 they killed Edward Johnson. I mean, you look back on it and you know, certainly, if I knew then what I know now I don't think he would have died. Um … it's very sad. You know, I'd just sat in the execution chamber and watched them gas the poor guy to death!

And whatever theoretical views one might have about the death penalty become very much humanised when you meet the people involved, when you watch some guy dying in front of you, who you actually rather like – it's obscene.

So yeah, I was angry and there are other things too, I had just come from talking with the family and I had to tell these poor people who had been trodden on all their lives that the government had just done it to them again.

And one of the fascinating things about having the BBC there, was it actually injected such a level of unreality – you kept thinking that someone was going to call 'Cut' and it was all going to be over. And thankfully, for Edward's sake, he believed that too.

When I went into the … I actually walked with him into the gas chamber and he said to me, 'Is there something you know that I don't know?' and I didn't quite understand what he meant to begin with, but I figured it out – that he really thought they weren't going to do it. And in that sense it was good to have the journalists.

It was horrendous for him, you know. It's frustrating later to discover this woman who had been with him at the time of the murder, who could have said that he couldn't have done it. But, you know, when I talk to her about why she didn't do anything, it actually illustrates the total powerlessness of someone in Edward's position and many of these other guys' position.

She said, 'Who am I gonna call? I can't call the FBI, it's not like in the movies where the FBI come swooping in to do the right thing.' And she said, 'Look, I went to the police, I told them he hadn't done it, and they told me to buzz off and mind my own business.'

And that's the ultimate powerlessness and, of course, it's true of so many poor people in Mississippi and elsewhere.

Well, it took forever. I mean, one thing is people always act like this is over instantaneously, it's absolute nonsense! They had him sitting in that chair for fifteen minutes. And if you think how long a minute can be if we just sit here in silence for a minute right now. You imagine if those was the last fifteen minutes of your life, it just went on and on and on.

And it was about halfway through that poor old Edward finally worked out that no one was going to call him. And, you know, he said, 'Well, let's get it over with.' And then what he goes through, you know, you always have these perverse discussions where the doctors say, 'Oh, don't try and hold your breath, that just makes it more painful.' Well, that's just not a human reaction, of course. And so, it took forever!

We'd raised a legal issue in Edward's case which the courts rejected, and then about ten years later the Supreme Court said we were right. And the Supreme Court said, 'Well, the best we can say is we were simply wrong in Edward Johnson's case.' But, you know, that's not much consolation because the guy's cold in his grave.

Well, I very rarely discuss why the death penalty's wrong, because it seems to me that is the wrong question. The real issue is – why is the death penalty right? What does it achieve?

And, you know, when I've watched people die, it's always at night and you come out of the execution chamber, and you look up at the stars and you say, 'Well, you know, how did that make the world a better place?' and it didn't, and it achieved absolutely nothing positive.

So we can argue about all these different things, about, you know, whether it's a deterrent or not – the guys I represented didn't know what deterrent means. Is it a way to save money? No, it's more expensive. Are we going to make mistakes? Of course we make mistakes.

I mean there are hundreds of intellectual arguments about why it's wrong, but I just think we don't need to go that far because no one can justify why it's right.

MR GOVE, MEET MR OGILVIE

2 JULY 2013

TODAY'S *INDEPENDENT* SPLASH is one of those where my inner saddo comes out, and I think: 'Hmmm, I hope they've thought about VAT.'

A very quick explanation for the few non-tax-experts out there.

The service of providing education is exempt from VAT – i.e. it's wholly outside the VAT system – because it's one of those which our European forefathers decided was either inappropriate or too complicated to tax, alongside banking, healthcare, burials and a few other things.

Incidentally, John Redwood once submitted a group of Parliamentary Questions asking how much money would be raised by taxing all of these exempt services. Oh what fun we had: 'The Tories want to make you pay VAT to bury your gran', etc. Happy days.

You might think being VAT-exempt is a good thing, but oh no, it's a terrible thing. If you're a high-street bank, you have to pay VAT on the electricity, heating, pens, paperclips, computers, telephones and all the other goods and services that you purchase in order to run your business. But because the service you provide is exempt from VAT, you can't pass this VAT onto your customers, nor can you claim the money back from HMRC.

Effectively, the banks are in the same position the public are in: they're the final consumer of the goods, and they're not charging VAT to anyone else, so the VAT bill sticks with them. For that reason, it's often referred to as 'sticky VAT'.

Now, obviously the government doesn't want the schools, hospitals and other bodies it funds to be stuck with large VAT bills each year, not least because it doesn't want them spending money on the sort of VAT avoidance schemes that all the banks engage in to get around the rules. So it operates a series of VAT refund schemes, all administered under Section 33 of the VAT Act 1994.

This means that most ordinary state schools simply tot up all the VAT bills they incur for the costs of providing their education, submit these to HMRC via the local authority, and get the money back. When academies (and later free schools) were introduced, a specific scheme was introduced for them to do likewise (nattily called Section 33B), to recognise they weren't getting their funds via the local authority.

So far, so good. The issue becomes if free schools or academies are allowed to have full financial freedom, and start effectively operating as profit-making businesses, in the same way that e.g. language colleges do.

Section 33 already provides for a distinction between the business and non-business activity of schools, but that's about them renting out their astroturf pitches to football teams; it's not about the core activity of providing education. But nevertheless, the principle is clear: the VAT refund scheme cannot apply when you are doing things to make money.

Unlike language schools, Gove and co. are not suggesting that free schools and academies should be able to charge pupils for the education they receive, so they could argue that the service of education will continue to be provided free of charge, and that Section 33B therefore remains justified to the extent it only refunds VAT incurred in providing that service.

But there's also an important point of principle: the existing VAT refund schemes (for schools, hospitals, local and police authorities, government departments and – thanks to Ed Miliband – national museums and galleries) only apply to non-profit-making bodies. I can't think of a single 'business' which benefits from those special schemes, and I can't imagine the lawyers in Brussels who police the EU VAT system taking it too kindly if they did.

And there's the basic issue of how these schools are going to make their money. If they effectively have a contractual relationship with the government – i.e. we receive your funding, and we use that money to provide education, facilities, and to make a profit on top, then it's not clear to me how they differ from G4S or any other private business that the government pays to deliver services. So why should the government also refund the VAT they incur?

At the very least, it's going to complicate a system which is currently pretty simple. At worst, if there is no sound legal basis to provide VAT refunds to a profit-making business, then the extra 20 per cent VAT bills that will stick with any free school or academy enjoying that status will blow a pretty big hole in the financial underpinning for Gove's master plan.

Which is why I hope someone from the Department for Education has consulted Mr David Ogilvie, the master civil servant who administers all the VAT refund schemes (if he hasn't moved on since we last met). And if they haven't yet done so, it might partly explain why some DfE officials are urging Gove to slow down a little on this plan and do his maths first.

HERE'S TO THREE STRIKES
TOMMY WATSON

5 JULY 2013

HAVING SPENT A large part of yesterday writing about Tommy Watson's two previous resignations for my book, today's announcement that he was stepping down as Ed M's election coordinator felt almost natural, as though we should all have been expecting it.

I was amazed to spend the day getting text messages and DMs from journalists, from Labour and Tory MPs, and from political consultants asking excitedly what it all meant, and what was going to happen next.

The reality is anyone who's resigned before is more likely to resign again, and anyone with two resignations to their credit is nailed on for a third. Why? Well, some of them – mentioning no names – are rather trouble-prone. But the likes of Tom have thrived on the periods they've spent out of the political front line, so it simply holds no fears for them. In fact, it holds massive attractions.

When he found himself in a situation over the last fortnight where he was back in the papers, people writing rubbish about him, his Twitter timeline clogged with trolls, and trouble-making Labour MPs and shadow Cabinet members trying to 'do him in', he did what any sensible person in his situation did, and said: 'Do you know what, folks, I don't need this, I'd be far happier doing my own thing without any of this bollocks.'

And while many people in politics say that to themselves in their heads but don't act on it because it feels like too much of a plunge, Tom's made that plunge before. He knows that plunge takes you into a lovely blue lagoon with no pressure, no worries, and lots of time to think, write, listen to music and drink banana daiquiris. So why wouldn't he? And write a fantasy resignation letter while he was at it.

Good on you, Tom, and this time – don't let them talk you back.

This was McBride's final blog article for almost a year. In the meantime, his book Power Trip *was published and, on returning to his job at CAFOD in October 2013, his employers barred him from any public activity, including blogging. He resumed his writing only after leaving CAFOD eight months later.*

FORTY WEEKS, FORTY DAYS:
A TIME FOR WARRIORS

19 JUNE 2014

TODAY MARKS FORTY weeks until the start of election purdah. After which, there will be just over forty days until the polls open.

So only forty weeks remain for ministers to take 'major decisions', announce 'new initiatives', or use taxpayers' money to puff their achievements.[20] Beyond that, the restrictions of purdah – the

---

20 Not that it stopped the Labour government doing all those things during the effort to save the Rover car plant in the middle of the 2005 election campaign, although technically, matters of national economic interest over-ride the restrictions of purdah, and the Tories were never going to argue otherwise.

old Persian word for 'curtain', used to denote the separation of male and female living quarters – will kick in, and the civil service will put its collective feet up until the election.

Even now, junior officials have 26 March 2015 marked in their calendars as the point when the veil will be drawn between politics and government. The more popular ministers will spend their last afternoons in the office drinking champagne with their civil servants and be clapped out of the door; others will hear the corks popping as they leave.[21]

Several other dates loom large before then which could significantly alter the election outlook: the outcome and aftermath of the hacking trials; the publication of Chilcot and the speech of his life that Ed Miliband will need to make in response; the monthly meetings of the Bank's increasingly hawkish Monetary Policy Committee; and above all, the eve-of-purdah Budget in March – when George Osborne will unveil the biggest immediate tax cut he can afford, and promise lots more in the future that he can't.

Alongside these set-piece moments, there are other critical imponderables that could at least shape the outcome on 7 May, if not dictate it. And I don't just mean parochial little issues like leaders' debates, Cabinet reshuffles, and whether Ed Miliband should appear on *Graham Norton*. I mean the things that Westminster dreads – uncontrollable events from afar or on high – floods, war, terrorism, Scotland's referendum and the impending, inescapable,

---

21 A memo to current ministers. Even if you're very popular, and your staff buy you lots of champagne, don't get lost in exuberance and leave a comedic 'welcome note' on your desk for your potential successor. It won't seem so funny when some gigantic shit like David Laws gets hold of it.

apocalyptic collapse of the global economy. The last two are not related.

But all those potential game-changing moments – planned and unplanned – can wait for another day. What matters most of all now is the mindset of the parties going into this forty-week, forty-day period.[22] And I don't mean amongst the foot-soldiers thanklessly working each day to build up voter ID in key marginals, but the mindset of the group at the top of each party to whom those soldiers will look to control the political agenda over the next forty weeks and give them some decent messages for the doorstep and the phone bank.

Every one of those weeks must be fought as a war, just as surely as every day of the campaign that will follow. For the next forty Mondays, the key generals in each party must sit down with their respective leaders and say: 'What are we going to say or do to win this week? What front will we attack on? And who will lead the

---

22 I was inspired to write this blog in a state of distress while watching the final hour of Day Two of the second Test between West Indies and New Zealand from Trinidad. You can keep the Brazil World Cup – that's my choice of a day of armchair sport. With only three wickets down, the Windies had two young batsmen set at the crease – Darren Bravo and Kraigg Brathwaite – both with centuries. They had the third-ranked batsman in the world, Shiv Chanderpaul, next up, plus their in-form captain Denesh Ramdin and young debutant Jermaine Blackwood also due in. So Bravo and Brathwaite had only one job left: to see off the new ball and make sure the Windies went into Day Three set fair to bat three sessions and build a first innings lead of at least 300. Instead, Bravo got himself out slogging the last over before the new ball was due, and Brathwaite popped a mistimed drive back to the bowler two overs before close of play. What that screamed out at me was the absence of a winning mindset. Having focused hard on reaching their personal milestones, they lacked the ability to see the wider context of the game and think what their team required of them; they lacked the concentration to keep winning the next ball and the next over and, ultimately, the match. That's not about skill or talent; it's about mindset. As in cricket, so in politics. Always.

fight?' And for the next forty Sundays, the same group needs to sit down and ask themselves honestly: 'Who won?'

The answer is never 'no one', not even a week dominated by Iraq and the World Cup, not even the five weekends in August when everyone will be on holiday. If no one appears to have won the week, then the winner is the party whom the status quo serves best, in terms of current public sentiment and voting intentions. I'd say that's Labour. Others may differ.

The point is that – at this stage in the electoral cycle – every week counts, and there needs to be a plan and a will to win it, along with a relentless determination not to be side-tracked or blown off course. Sometimes external factors make that inevitable, but if minds are properly focused in this way, it should at least make self-inflicted wounds easier to avoid, and increase the hunger to feast on the other side's mistakes.

As General Patton told the Fourth Army a fortnight and seventy years ago: 'There are 400 neatly marked graves somewhere in Sicily. All because one man went to sleep on the job. But they are German graves, because we caught the bastard asleep before they did.'

Every week lost because someone goes to sleep on the job is a week won by the other side. By the same token, if there are people within any party who are still too busy fighting their own battles or, even worse, planning for future elections to come, not the one in 322 days' time, then they need to be locked in a House of Commons cupboard with Phil Neville until the war is over. Or at least a fortnight at a time until they've learnt their lesson.

So what is the state of war-readiness at the top of the three major parties? Well, for different reasons and to different degrees – as Patton found with the Fourth Army – they all need some whipping into shape.

The morale of Tory troops is high after the Euro and Newark elections, and rightly so: their ground game and resulting performance was much better than anyone expected, apart from the irrepressible Grant Shapps, who masterminded it all. But for all the unity, discipline and sense of purpose amongst backbenchers, party activists and Shapps's team, where the hell is it at Cabinet level, with Gove, May and their advisers knocking the shit out of each other, and Cameron starting battles he can't win in Europe?

At the top, the Tory mindset currently looks dangerously like Labour's in the run-up to the 2005 election. Half the Cabinet complacently assume that victory is inevitable because they're complacent about the economy, complacent about Ed Miliband, complacent about Scotland, and complacently confuse their popularity with the media and their MPs for what the public think of them. Let's call them the complacent ones.

The other, pessimistic, half look at Lord Ashcroft's polling and scratch their heads wondering how on earth the current projections are going to add up to a Tory majority and David Cameron continuing as their leader.

Both sides are therefore allowing their attention to drift beyond the next election, which – like 2005 – is a real toss-up at this stage, and focusing instead on what may happen afterwards. Labour left it dangerously late to get its act together at the top in 2005, and the Tories can't afford to do the same.

As for the Lib Dems, the ground game is all they've got, so they're lucky it's a half-decent one. Quite what they do at the top about their manifesto, messaging and messengers is a mystery, and getting them into a united, winning mindset will require a miracle. But at least after the recent elections, they know what doesn't work.

As things stand, and barring radical change, the Lib Dem headquarters in Great George Street is the Maginot Line of war-readiness, destined only for obsolescence. If they win even one of the next forty weeks, even their own party conference in Glasgow, I'll be amazed.

Then there's Labour, where the current mindset problem is more simple and more easily resolved. Put bluntly, it's hard for the generals to sit down and plan how to win each week when Labour currently has no generals.

There are many positive things to say about the people managing Ed Miliband's operation and running Labour's campaign. They are well-spoken, well-read, well-connected and, if you stay on their right side, quite genial. You'd feel safe sitting them next to your mum at a wedding.

But what they are not is fighters. They will never give their press team and foot-soldiers the ammunition required to win the next forty weeks in the media and on the doorstep, not just because they lack an understanding of what might do the trick, but also because they lack an appreciation of why doing so matters. Not when they could be attending a Thomas Piketty symposium instead.

Just like David Cameron, Ed Miliband has been guilty of recruiting his innermost circle of advisers entirely in his own image. That's alright in peacetime if it helps him shape his political philosophy and refine his personal blueprint for government. It might even be OK if basking in a large majority in office.

But with an election to win – an election Labour can win – Ed urgently needs to add some 'wartime consiglieres' to the mix, not in place of the very capable and trusted people he's got, but working alongside them.

If that creates tensions and fissures – as it clearly did during the recent election campaign, when characters like that found themselves ignored and artlessly briefed against by the inner circle – then he needs to put one person in charge whom all sides will accept and respect. If Mandelson won't do it, then I dunno – what's Fraser Kemp up to these days?

What's more, Ed needs to break down the purdah he has created within his own shadow Cabinet, with a handful of close, like-minded, unchallenging allies sitting with him on one side of the curtain and the majority twiddling their thumbs on the other side waiting to be told what's going on.

Within the latter group, there are at least a dirty dozen of battle-hardened soldiers you'd always want in the trenches with you: 'Balls, Benn, Burnham, Coaker, Cooper, Creagh…' That's not a bad start to the morning roll-call, and yet where are they and the others from D to W at present? In the reserve lines, awaiting orders.

In contrast to David Cameron, Ed Miliband's Labour Party is genuinely blessed with countless advisers, MPs and top shadow ministers who not only – to quote Patton again – 'love the sting and clash of battle', but know exactly what war needs to be fought and won each week of the year ahead. The problem is that none of them are currently managing Ed Miliband's operation or leading Labour's campaign. And that needs fixing fast.

From this point on, every week is a war, and every leader needs his warriors up front.

OK THEN, ANSWER ME THIS...

24 JUNE 2014

GIVEN THE FACT that – the moment the verdict on Andy Coulson was announced in the House of Commons – George Osborne began using the 'Aha, what about Damian McBride?' defence, it's safe to assume this is what's known as the 'line to take' for the Tories, and doubtless we'll hear it again when David Cameron makes his own 'apology' to the House of Commons.

Let's forget for a moment the whole business of equating my behaviour – however reprehensible – with the criminal activities for which Andy Coulson has just been convicted. If others want to get exercised about that, then be my guest. I believe a far more important point needs to be made.

When I was employed by Gordon Brown as his Head of Communications at the Treasury, it was on the back of an unimpeachable and pretty successful seven years working as a civil servant. There was no reason at all for concern about how I was going to do that job, hence Gus O'Donnell interviewing and recommending me for the role.

Nevertheless, to prove that there were no reasons for concern, I had to undergo the developed vetting process, and have my finances, love life and past activities thoroughly looked through by the security services. I was not allowed to start doing the job properly until I'd received my DV status. And, as I wrote two years ago, 'I'd defy anyone to go through that process and come through with their secrets still hidden.'

So was Gordon wrong to employ me, or make me his political press adviser two years later, or take me with him in that role to Downing Street two years after that? With the benefit of a huge slice of hindsight, the answer might be 'yes' to all the above, but – at the time those decisions were made – there was absolutely no reason not to, whatever 'warnings' various people now claim that they sounded, which is why all three appointments were utterly uncontroversial.

Now, look at Andy Coulson. When he was employed by George Osborne and David Cameron as the Tory Head of Communications, it was on the back of having to resign as *News of the World* editor after Clive Goodman and Glenn Mulcaire were convicted of phone hacking. It was a hugely controversial appointment, as was making him No. 10's Director of Communications even after severe doubts had been raised about the 'one rogue reporter' defence that Coulson had maintained since leaving the *News of the World*.

Their explanation is that they believed in second chances, they trusted Coulson's assurances that there was nothing more to 'come out' about him, there were no complaints about the way he did his job in CCHQ or No. 10, and so – even if it has ultimately proved a bad call to employ him – it was the wrong judgement made for all the right reasons.

But here's the problem. There's a reason the developed vetting process exists, and similar services provided by private firms to organisations like the Tory Party: it's to take the subjectivity out of potentially risky or highly sensitive appointments; it's to ensure that two nice blokes like Dave and George don't have to feel embarrassed asking their mate Andy whether he's still receiving payments from his old employers, or whether he's had a sexual relationship with any newspaper editors, or whether he's telling the truth when he says he knew nothing about phone hacking.

If those questions were never asked, or if that kind of vetting process was conveniently and inexplicably side-stepped when Coulson went to No. 10, then that ceases to be an issue of judgement, and instead becomes something more serious.

So if the Tories want to keep using the 'What about Damian McBride?' line, then so be it, but they cannot then dodge the follow-up question: 'Fine, if you want to make that comparison, why was Coulson not put through developed vetting for the Director of Communications job in No. 10 when McBride was for a far more junior job in the Treasury?'

THE ART OF
BLOCKING EU
APPOINTMENTS

27 JUNE 2014

C LEARLY, DAVID CAMERON is never going to take any advice from Gordon Brown, let alone from me or my book. But if he's unsuccessful today in his full-frontal assault on Jean-Claude Juncker, he may wish he'd at least listened to the great Sir Jon Cunliffe in advance. Jon is now bringing his wisdom to bear at the Bank of England, but in his old Treasury and No. 10 days, he was Gordon's key adviser on European matters, and helped him to many of his unlikely triumphs in Brussels.[23]

One of those, as detailed on p. 140–41 of my book, involved Gordon trying to block the planned appointment of the Franco-German candidate and overwhelming favourite for a major post. Sound familiar? In this case, the candidate was French banking technocrat Jean Lemierre and the job was Head of the IMF back in the spring of 2004.

Did Gordon go in full guns blazing, criticising Lemierre's credentials and opinions, threatening to veto his appointment etc.? Of course not. Instead, he successfully persuaded his fellow finance ministers at their Dublin summit that – in the interests of a transparent and fair process – they should first have a discussion about the attributes they were looking for in any nominee for the role, and then weigh up all the potential candidates against those criteria.

All eminently sensible and impossible to disagree with. No table-thumping or threats required, and certainly no personal attacks on Lemierre liable to make the French and German politicians and press defensive on his behalf. Next, Gordon skilfully steered the discussion to recognise a number of attributes that Lemierre didn't have in his locker, but that other candidates did. Again, all reasonable and impossible to disagree with.

---

23 Incidentally, it was often observed that – even though they were present at hundreds of the same summits over the years – you never, ever saw Jon Cunliffe and Jean-Claude Juncker in the same room together. Speculation was rife amongst his Treasury colleagues – not least Gordon – that JC and J-C were in fact the same person, and this explained why Jon always had such impeccable intelligence on what the French and Germans were thinking. It's never been denied by 'either' party.

As the meeting ended without a decision, Gordon then – via me – arranged a planted question for the press conference that followed on the issue of 'what kind of candidate are you looking for?' and helpfully provided Irish Finance Minister Charlie McCreevy with his summary of the attributes agreed at the meeting. Charlie answered, and the verdict of the media was clear: Lemierre was toast, and Gordon's favoured alternative – Spain's Rodrigo Rato – was the new favourite.

Mission accomplished, but at no stage before or afterwards was this presented as the UK's demand or Gordon's triumph. It was just damn good successful diplomacy, and no one was left feeling a loser, except poor Jean Lemierre. Obviously, in contrast to David Cameron, it helped that Gordon had an alternative candidate in mind and on the table, but ultimately, it was the approach that mattered.

In the absence of Gordon, Jon Cunliffe or myself, if Cameron does want to listen to someone who was there that day in Dublin for advice on how to handle these types of negotiations, he could always ask one Jean-Claude Juncker. J-CJ was there in his capacity as Luxembourg's Finance Minister, and as a Lemierre supporter, I'm sure he remembers it well. Maybe he could tell the story to Dave later in the spirit of 'some you win, some you lose' – I'm sure that would go down a treat.

SOME MISSING WORDS ON EUROPE

30 JUNE 2014

E D MILIBAND GAVE a good attacking performance in the House of Commons earlier, but for me, he missed a massive trick. This is the section I think he should have included:

> And yes, the last Labour government – and Tony Blair in particular – made many mistakes on Europe. Tony Blair was wrong to agree a new financial arrangement which meant a reduction in Britain's rebate. He was wrong to accept enlargement without accompanying reforms of the rules on free movement of labour and on welfare. He was wrong not to insist on longer transition arrangements for the new entrants to the EU. And he was wrong

to agree the Lisbon Treaty without giving the British people the referendum they were promised … And, while I'm at it, so was the current Prime Minister.

Tony Blair made most of those mistakes after 2002. He did so to try to compensate for Britain's decision on the Euro and for Britain's isolation on Iraq. He bent over backwards trying to make friends in Europe – even at the expense of Britain's national interest – and that is always, always the wrong thing to do. But so is going out of your way to try to make enemies, again at the expense of Britain's national interest, and that is what today's Prime Minister stands guilty of.

My policy is clear: Britain's national interest will always come first, and the British people will always have the final word on any decisions that matter. But – when I want to secure what's best for Britain – I will build alliances in Europe, I will lead from the front in Europe, and I will win the arguments in Europe, because that's what's works.

Now, there are all sorts of reasons Ed Miliband can't say anything that critical of Tony Blair, but – with the publication of Chilcot approaching – both Ed and all the most zealous Blairite MPs and supporters are going to have to get used to it. And, much more importantly, Europe is an issue where the Labour leadership has to stop judging things by what the party and its Europhile tendency can stomach, but on whether what it's saying makes sense to the British public.

Now, about that in/out referendum…

HAVE YOU NO SENSE
OF DECENCY, HARRIET?

7 JULY 2014

McBride reacted strongly to a report in the Standard *that Harriet Harman was planning to accuse Gordon Brown of 'sexism' at a parliamentary event that evening.*

I T TAKES A lot to get me angry these days. Three years working amongst the saintly staff of CAFOD beat most of the red mist out of me, and – sport aside – I nowadays react to most blows with stoical calm, even attacks on Gordon Brown. But whether it's withdrawal symptoms from CAFOD or today's steamy weather,

Harriet Harman's plan to accuse Gordon of sexism in Parliament tonight has got me rather irked.

First, there's the motive – cynical even by my own old standards. What Harriet wants to do is pave the way to attack the belated appointment of more women to David Cameron's Cabinet on Monday as 'window-dressing' (she's even helpfully included that Caroline Flint quote in her speech, just in case we'd forgotten the reference). But she doesn't want that to look too obvious or too partisan, so she's trying to make it look like a wider attack on the political culture in general, and there's no easier dog to kick in her own garden than Gordon Brown.

Second, there's the casual nature of the sexism charge. Being accused of sexism is no different from being accused of racism or homophobia: they're the preserve of the prejudiced and pig-ignorant; their ilk are responsible for the worst crimes on earth. Those are not accusations to throw around lightly, and you'd better have damn good evidence to make them. Especially if you're accusing someone like Gordon Brown, who has had an utterly unblemished record for decades of appointing men and women to the most senior roles in his civil service staff, his special adviser units and his ministerial teams, and working alongside them with never the slightest suggestion of differentiation based on their gender. In fact, as I said earlier on Twitter, Gordon divides the world into only two categories: useless and not useless; that is the only basis on which he judges anyone.

So third, let's look at the evidence Harriet offers. Item 1: When she won Labour's deputy leadership, she says there was a row over whether she would be called the Deputy Prime Minister. You're damn right there was, and it had absolutely nothing to do with her gender. We had decided in advance that no matter who won the deputy leadership, male or female, we didn't want them styling themselves as the Deputy PM, or assuming they'd inherit the responsibilities and trappings that went with that. If Alan Johnson had won, we'd have done the same. Item 2: When the G20 summit was held in London, she was invited to a dinner with the spouses of the world leaders. Again, absolutely true, but this time, it was to do with her gender. Sarah Brown had decided to turn the dinner into a grand Downing Street event for Britain's leading women from all walks of life; and Harriet – as one of those – was invited. The problem is Harriet seems to think she should have been invited to the leaders' dinner instead, or perhaps to the meetings of the G20. To which I'd respectfully ask … erm, why? What on earth would Harriet have contributed to the meetings and dinner where Gordon, Obama, Sarkozy and Merkel were hammering out the global financial stimulus to bring the world out of recession? I mean seriously, what? But if she thinks she was excluded from those discussions because of her gender, Harriet needs to remind herself that Gordon's key adviser throughout those meetings was Baroness Shriti Vadera. Why? Because she was the world expert on what needed to happen. With all due respect, Harriet was not.

Fourth and finally, there's the timing of all this. Harriet is accusing Gordon of being a sexist at a time when he is putting his own full weight and the resources of his Global Campaign for Education foundation into leading the effort to free the schoolgirls kidnapped by Boko Haram in northern Nigeria, and to try to prevent a similar fate befalling other children in the region. He's not just doing so because of a natural concern for the fate of those individual schoolgirls, but because of a fundamental belief that the education of girls is the key that unlocks all other doors to tackling world poverty, and that any assault on the right of girls to education, whether in Nigeria or Afghanistan, must be fought by the whole world. Gordon could have chosen any issue to focus on in the aftermath of his time in office. He chose that one.

To call that man a sexist is not only wrong but shameful, and to do so as mere collateral in the search for some narrow partisan gain next Monday is frankly beneath the office of Labour's deputy leader.

This article brought an equally strong response from Ms Harman, saying McBride had been sacked from government for denigrating women and was doing so again.

WILL I BE GASCOIGNE
OR CANIGGIA?

12 JULY 2014

FOR THE UNFORTUNATE ones who remember it, tomorrow's World Cup decider between Germany and Argentina conjures up memories of their last final meeting in Rome in the summer of 1990, a dreadful encounter which saw the Argies reduced to nine men by the end, and West Germany winning by a late Andreas Brehme penalty.

It could all have been so different. I don't mean the Ireland vs Cameroon final that all right-thinking romantics were dreaming of at the quarter-final stage. But if Claudio Caniggia had not been suspended for the game against West Germany, Argentina would surely have played with a bit more adventure and pace, and troubled an ageing German defence.

Caniggia was one of the stars of the Italia '90 World Cup, capturing the eye with his mane of blond hair and his direct running style, seen to spectacular effect in Argentina's shock opening game defeat by Cameroon, when one of his trademark runs was brought to a halt by Benjamin Massing in what remains one of the greatest moments in World Cup history.

Thankfully, after Caniggia's body was glued back together, he went on to play a crucial role in Argentina's progress, scoring the only goal of their Last 16 game against Brazil, and then delivering one of the best headed finishes you'll ever see to equalise in the semi-final against hosts Italy.

But it's what happened after that for which Claudio Caniggia should always be remembered. At 1–1 in the dying minutes of normal time, with Argentina hanging on and Caniggia ploughing a lone furrow up front, he leapt to reach a high clearance on halfway, and was harshly booked for deliberate handball.

It was his second yellow of the tournament. If Argentina made it to the final, he would not play. He looked dumbstruck for about two seconds. He protested to the ref. But then he got on with it. No crying. No internal meltdown. No Maradona pointing at the bench saying, 'Have a word.'

Instead, he ran his socks off for the last minutes of the game and all of extra time, chasing hopeless causes and eating seconds off the clock, especially after Argentina had a man sent off. When the match went to penalties, he put himself forward, and would have taken Argentina's fifth if they'd needed it.

In short, he gave one of the all-time classic displays of putting the team first rather than thinking about himself. And of course, the following night in Turin, when Paul Gascoigne was booked in England's semi-final against West Germany, we then saw the exact opposite – right down to Gazza's refusal to take a penalty, fatefully leaving the job to Chris Waddle instead.

There was no difference between Caniggia and Gascoigne in age or experience. The difference was all in their heads: one a total team player, the other a devout prima donna.

We saw more Caniggia-style heroics when Andy Moeller was booked in the semi-final of Euro '96 against England, and yet revelled in scoring the winning penalty to send his team-mates through to the final. And perhaps most magnificent of all was Roy Keane's display in that same Turin stadium in 1999, driving Manchester United on to their comeback victory in the Champions League semi-final second leg against Juventus after receiving the booking that would put him out of the final.

As in football, so in life. Just like Caniggia and Gascoigne, both aged twenty-three, facing identical situations one night apart in Italy, we all face choices about how we react to setbacks and knocks.

Sometimes our reaction is to knuckle down, think about what's best for the team and those around us, and play our part in the broader success; to think, 'I've worked bloody hard to get us to this point, and – just because I'm feeling bent out of shape – I'll be buggered if I stop doing my bit now.'

But sometimes our reaction is to think only about ourselves, to sulk and flounce around; to think, 'If I'm not getting what I want out of this, then sod the rest, sod doing my bit, because I'm the only thing that matters.'

I speak as someone who invariably makes the wrong choice; I can be a right bloody Gascoigne even at the best of times, and especially in the heat of the moment. And the hardest thing is that when we face those crunch moments, we don't usually have time to think coolly or rationally about our response.

When a minister gets a phone call from No. 10 on Monday giving them disappointing news about the reshuffle, they'll have to make instant decisions about how to react, what to say, whether to agree, and many of them will regret those decisions just an hour later.

To them, to myself, to all of us, I'd just say: remember that Claudio Caniggia and Paul Gascoigne had only two or three seconds to decide how they were going to react to their yellow cards, on the biggest stage either of them would ever play,[24] with hundreds of millions watching around the world and the sporting fortunes of their nations at stake.

So when you next face a setback like that, and have your own two or three seconds to decide whether you go one way or the other, and many years afterwards to live with the consequences, just take that time to ask yourself: Am I going to be Gascoigne or Caniggia?

---

24 Coincidentally, both men went on to wind down their careers playing for Glasgow Rangers FC, a once prominent Scottish football side which was sadly disbanded in 2012.

ITV vs BBC =
GERMANY vs ARGENTINA

13 JULY 2014

WHEN I WAS born forty years ago in the middle of the 1974 World Cup, the choice between watching the final on BBC or ITV remained one of the great dilemmas of our time.

Like Wizzard vs Slade for Christmas No. 1 in 1973; I mean, how could anyone choose between Christmas for 'Everybody' or Christmas 'Everyday'? Like Jack Nicholson's Jake Gittes vs Al Pacino's Michael Corleone for Best Actor in 1975; both inexplicably beaten by the BT Sport candidate, Art Carney.

Over the years, once I gained control of the remote, I wrestled with the BBC vs ITV choice myself. Brian Moore and Big Ron always had to be preferable to John Motson and Bobby Charlton; but then Des Lynam could knock Elton Welsby into a cocked hat with not a hair of his 'tache out of place. And what to do when the BBC finally allowed the sainted Barry Davies to do the final in 1994, or when ITV poached Des in 2002?

But roll forward to this year's 'dilemma', and it's suddenly become Morecambe vs Wise, Ali vs Foreman, Mariah Carey vs bloody East 17. I mean, the anti-advertising, antediluvian masses aside, is there any right-thinking person who would choose the BBC over ITV for coverage of the final?

Let's start in the commentary box. Guy Mowbray and Mark Lawrenson vs Clive Tyldesley and Andy Townsend. I've nothing against Mowbray and I'm no Tyldesley fanatic, but in terms of big game presence, I'm going to go with the guy who's been doing the biggest Champions League games for the past umpteen years. He knows what to do.

But it's the co-commentary choice which is really stark. Lawrenson has been a disgrace in this World Cup, paid to be there out of our licence fees but treating the whole experience like a toilet attendant in Magaluf. The BBC should have bitten the bullet and replaced him for the final with Danny Murphy or Martin Keown, but – as Barry Davies always found – seniority is king at the Beeb.

By contrast, Andy Townsend commentates with verve and passion, kicking every ball, grabbing every cheat by the collar, willing the game to get better. Lawrenson's reaction to a dull game is to wish he was on the beach; Townsend reacts as if he wants to be on the pitch.

Then we have the contest in the studio. And it's here that the match between Argentina and Germany is a parallel of the BBC v. ITV. Argentina have Messi and nothing else. Ditto the BBC and Gary Lineker. Lineker is a lovely man to have in your living room: he's a warm host and an acerbic, witty analyst all in one; but he's trying to do it all on his own, and – like Messi – it's not enough to win.

And here's my sole criticism of him: the mark of a great presenter is bringing the best out of his panellists. Lineker has some strong material to work with: Alan Hansen is in his swansong year and used to be very good; Thierry Henry is a natural; ditto Ruud Gullit. Yet all of them have lapsed into the same turgid torpor that is the natural preserve of Alan Shearer. Turn the sound down and – Robbie Savage aside – you'd think they were commentating on a floodlight failure. And, ultimately, that failure lies at Lineker's door, even if he wasn't responsible for booking Clarence Seedorf.

We then switch to ITV, and it's like a kid of my vintage turning from *Take Hart* to *Tiswas*. Lee Dixon, Martin O'Neill, Gordon Strachan, Ian Wright, Glenn Hoddle – all of them opinionated, argumentative, energetic, funny – and their natural style in turn bringing out the best from Paddy Vieira and Fabio Cannavaro. That's the German team right there: if Muller doesn't get you, Kroos will, and God help you when they all attack as one.

And, right at the heart of it, we have Adrian Chiles: the Bastian Schweinsteiger of this outfit, pulling the strings and unleashing the creative talent. Chiles has done what no one has ever success-fully done since Des Lynam in his '90s heyday: he's become the armchair fan sitting on the elite panel, asking the questions we'd ask, making the points we'd make and getting the best out of his panel in a way only someone with his background in sofa telly and talk radio ever could. It's been a masterful performance, a man at the top of his game, and to do it all while missing Roy Keane is even more impressive.

So it'll be ITV for me for the final, and if I have to sit through that awful Pot Noodle beach commercial one more time, so be it – it'll be a damn sight more colourful and entertaining than Alan Shearer's half-time thoughts.

WHAT IS POINT, RESHUFFLE?

14 JULY 2014

I F YOU KNOW the Radio 4 spoof phone-in show *Down the Line*, you'll recall Paul Whitehouse's character Khalid, who – whatever the topic under discussion, from the monarchy to marathon-running – would come on and ask the same nihilist question: 'What is point?'

Whatever explanation was offered by host Gary Bellamy (Rhys Thomas) to a question like 'What is point, Queen?', Khalid would dig deeper: 'What is point, tradition?', 'What is point, tourists?'[25]

---

25 Khalid's calls culminated in one of the greatest punch lines you'll ever hear, during a discussion about sport and horse-racing. Work it out.

The Khalid Test is a useful one to apply in politics whenever a minister wants to make some knee-jerk or attention-seeking announcement. And I find myself asking it about that relatively rare thing in British politics we expect to see this week: a discretionary reshuffle, not one prompted by a resignation, a bad election result, or a new leader. So, David Cameron: what is point, reshuffle?

You want some fresh faces in the Cabinet. You want some members of the 2010 intake to lower the average age. You want some more varied accents. And you particularly want some more women. You want all this not because you want fresh thinking or different perspectives in the Cabinet or in government departments – you've left it far too late for that in terms of the election – but just because you hope this lot will look and sound better than the current lot on the TV and radio. As Lord Ashcroft said yesterday on Twitter: this is all about optics.

To which our friend Khalid would say: 'What is point, optics?' I would be amazed if a single person in the country will change their vote at the next election because they suddenly start to see more of Steve Barclay, Therese Coffey or Kwasi Kwarteng on the news. They're all great, but they should have been in the Cabinet two years ago with time to make their mark, not as a sudden afterthought at this stage. Right now, new faces will do nothing for the Tories without time for new thinking and new policies.

To use a World Cup analogy, the only point of a reshuffle at this stage is to change the game. Fresh legs would be fine if the Tories were ahead or holding onto a draw but, right now, they're not. If Cameron really believes this reshuffle is necessary and will make a difference, then it must deliver a proper change in tactics – not just optics – similar to Gordon bringing Mandelson back to run the show in October 2008 or (very nearly) sacking Darling for Balls in 2009.

So what would be the game-changing moves to make this a worthwhile reshuffle and provide a satisfactory answer to answer Khalid's question?

1. Move Osborne
    I know, I know, you think I'm mad. But if George is the supreme tactician we're assured he is, even he would agree with my reasoning, and would willingly accept his new job as Tory election coordinator.
    This would be Dave's narrative:

    > George has been a brilliant austerity Chancellor – tough, ruthless and fearless – getting us through the hard times and laying the foundations of our long-term economic plan. Now what I want is a Chancellor whose priority will be the small businesses and ordinary families who will be the engine of growth and bedrock of our society in the years to come. And that's why I've put 'X' in charge for the last year of this Parliament.

All a load of cobblers, I know, but at least it sounds like Dave. But why would he do it? Because – and I know it's a hurtful thing to say – George just isn't very popular. His competence ratings have improved since 2012 cos, y'know, we're not in recession any more, but people made their mind up about him during the first two years of the Parliament, all culminating in the Omnishambles Budget when he confirmed every bad opinion.

What the Tories need is someone to deliver Budget 2015 – the real potential pre-election game-changer – who the public quite like. Ken Clarke could easily do it but he's a step back. Grant Shapps has the life story but he's one for the future. So the answer is simple: move William Hague to No. 11, simultaneously paving the way for Osborne to take over the Foreign Office at some point post-election.

2. Sack Gove

Let's be clear. One of the reasons that Dave has decided to do his 'optics' reshuffle is that he's constantly being told by Lynton Crosby's focus groups that he's seen as a posh tit presiding over a Cabinet of his posh tit mates. Sorry not to sugar-coat that, but that's what the focus groups say. The reshuffle he's currently planning will do nothing to challenge that perception, but sacking Michael Gove – the biggest preening tit of the lot – would be a genuinely bold and attention-grabbing move. And here's Dave's narrative, which – again – I'm sure a strategic genius like Gove would accept:

> Look, I want a united team going into the election, Michael's been a bit of a divisive presence in the past year, and I'd like to move beyond that. But, much more important, I govern for

the whole country; I don't want to divide people against each other. And when I hear Michael saying the teachers who disagree with him are bad, and the teachers who agree with him are good, well, I'm sorry, that's not what I want from my Education Secretary.

Give the job to Esther McVey, and tell her to spend the next ten months trying to win back the teachers who have deserted the Tories during Gove's reign. As for Gove, tell him to take a year's sabbatical, learn some humility and come back for a fresh challenge next Parliament.

3. Restore Foxy

The last change is simplest of all. Bring Liam Fox back as Foreign Secretary to take the place of William Hague. The public know him; he's a big, serious figure; and he could do what no one else would be capable of in the next ten months – least of all the genteel Hague – turning foreign policy into a proper election issue.

The public doesn't have to agree with Foxy's neo-con, interventionist rhetoric; what matters is that he takes a strong, clear stance and is not afraid to shout about it. And the Tories need the public to contrast that with a Labour leadership which ties itself in knots on every foreign policy issue from Libya to the EU referendum.

Foxy would make mincemeat of Douglas Alexander and whoever the Lib Dems put up in a pre-election debate, and there aren't many Cabinet ministers who could be similarly confident of winning their own battle right now, including Dave himself.

Hague in No. 11 in time for the big 2015 Budget, Gove's war against teachers ended, and Foxy back in the big time. In the process, two of Dave's posh mates sidelined, and advancement given to three of his non-mates with non-posh accents. Now there's a reshuffle with a point.

In the event, William Hague did leave the Foreign Office but not to take the place of George Osborne; Michael Gove was indeed moved from his Education brief to Chief Whip; and Liam Fox turned down an offer to return to a more junior position at the Foreign Office.

HOSTAGES, RODS AND WREATHS

4 AUGUST 2014

There was controversy when pictures emerged of the wreaths laid by party leaders at a First World War memorial service, David Cameron's written by himself and signed in his name, but Ed Miliband's (similar to other party leaders') bearing the inscription: 'From the Leader of the Opposition', written by the organisers.

WROTE AT THE weekend that Ed Miliband's recent speech on his lack of interest in image and photo ops was the most colossal hostage to fortune, which will be hung round his neck at some inopportune moment before the next election, when he is seen to be acting in exactly the opposite way.

And here's the problem: he knows that, and his team knows that. Every member of his staff will be petrified of being the one caught doing something out of concern for how the pictures will look. It won't matter that they're some junior monkey acting on their own initiative; the headlines about Ed's hypocrisy won't bother with the fine details. The trouble is – whisper it quietly – politicians, like any other public figures, do need people to check what is going to happen when they turn up at a particular venue, who they're going to meet, and what the pictures are going to look like. That's just basic good preparation. Some politicians' teams take it to extremes – George Osborne's Thea Rogers is particularly notorious for her Kubrick-style control of the Chancellor's visits. But done correctly and unobtrusively, it's also a good courtesy to your hosts, a helpful service for any accompanying media, and – most importantly – prevents all manner of screw-ups without anyone noticing. Gordon's 'advance' people over the years – civil servants like Helen Etheridge and Balshen Izzet, or party officials like Rachel Kinnock and Jo Dipple – were masters of the art. That brings us to today's incident with the wreaths at the Cenotaph. If I had to take a wild guess, I'd suggest that whoever did the 'advance' for David Cameron – with the experience of many Remembrance Sundays in Whitehall – asked what was happening with the messages for the wreaths. Having been told he'd be provided with one saying 'From the Prime Minister' or shown what it looked like, I'm guessing they said: 'Don't worry, he'll write a personal message; we'll let you have it in the next hour.'

Does that mean the PM is obsessed with image and photo ops? Not really, it just means he's got a team around him doing their jobs.[26]

Did Ed Miliband's team really forget to have that conversation with the ceremony organisers? Was the first any of them knew about the message on the wreath really when it was handed to their leader thirty seconds before he had lay it? And is their operation really as lacklustre and resigned to their fate as Nick Clegg's, who did the same thing?

Or is it a more serious problem: that the fear of being the first to screw up after Miliband's image speech means even the most effective staffers are scared to do their jobs properly, especially on an issue as sensitive as commemorating the war dead?

Ed's speech was indeed a massive hostage to fortune which will come back to haunt him at some stage in the future; but in the meantime, every day he tries to do the job as Leader of the Opposition out in public, it is a massive rod for his own back.

---

26 Incidentally, this row has obscured yet another example of our Prime Minister's horrific ignorance of history. Liberty? Liberty? In what way was the First World War about protecting 'our liberty'? Tell that to the Indian, African and Irish soldiers sent back after the war to colonial subjugation. Tell it to their ANZAC brothers forced to their deaths in a war that had nothing to do with them. Tell it to the Turks who fought against them to defend their own liberty. Above all, try to explain precisely what the connection was between the millions of British soldiers killed and maimed in the First World War, who we rightly remember and mourn this year, and the liberty that we enjoy in Britain today. Do not justify or celebrate their senseless slaughter with an appeal which only belongs to the great and noble sacrifice of their sons and daughters twenty-five years later in the war against fascism. You giant ignoramus.

BARBARA MCBRIDE:
A EULOGY PART ONE

8 AUGUST 2014

T HIS WAS THE eulogy that my brother Ben gave for my mum at her funeral mass at St Joseph's RC Church, Highgate, yesterday. She died in the Highgate Nursing Home nearby on 19 July. My own footnotes are below:

Barbara Halpin was born less than a mile from the Bow Bells: a true Cockney.

Her family was evacuated from the city bombs to the grounds of Knebworth House during World War Two, but Mum's London roots caused a small controversy in the village.

She had been entered into a parish princess competition, and won! But some locals told her parents it was not right that a girl from out of the village could take the crown.

So she retired from show business wiser but undefeated, aged about three, and from the time she got back to London, she would leave that tough path in life to her future classmate, Barbara Windsor.

Mum now showed other strengths: she won a school prize for an essay on Dickens – tickets to a Tchaikovsky concert.

When she got back from the concert, she showed her instinct for equality – a big cause throughout her life – by reflecting to a kind nun at school that she couldn't believe that God would not allow Tchaikovsky and his music into Heaven just because he loved a man not a woman.[27]

She met her friends for life at school: Jennifer, Marilyn, Mabs and Yvonne.

Mum really enjoyed her early working life as a nanny in Nice. Back in England, she dated a man from Texas, and had her first child with him, my brother Chris. But when work called him home and he proposed raising Chris in Texas, Mum preferred they stay in London close to her family, and they parted ways amicably.

---

27 My own favourite memory of Mum standing up against prejudice was when a stand-in priest at our local church, St Alban's, warned in his sermon that if we did not start increasing vocations from young British and Irish men, it would not be long until the only new priests would be coming from Africa and it would be a black priest standing in his place. He had barely returned to the vestry after Mass before Mum was back there telling him he was a disgrace and was never welcome in our church again.

She next studied Classics at Senate House. One day on campus, a young Glaswegian – Eugene McBride – said to his companion, John: 'Who's that blonde?'

'That blonde', said John, 'is my sister!' A spot of luck for Eugene, as John lived with Mum and was able to introduce them.

Dad showed he was keen by always studying opposite her in the library and regularly proposing marriage. After she finally accepted, they and Chris went to Canada for a few years but I think the cold winters there and missing her friends and family in London drew her back.

By then Mum had had the second of her children who went on to remarkable things: Nick. There was a car sticker in the '80s that read: 'If you can read this, thank a teacher', and Mum used to say: 'Yes, you can thank me!' There was a tree in our back garden in Finchley under which she taught Nick, me and Damian to read.

I should have concentrated harder, as – led by Chris – my three brothers would go on to study and even teach at Oxbridge colleges, work with Judges, Lords and Prime Ministers and, later, write books, which were of course dedicated to Mum.

She also nurtured students throughout her career teaching Latin and Classics at London secondary schools.

She would say to my Dad, a fellow teacher but one who could be more pessimistic about his students' attitude: 'If you just find one whose life you change, then you have done a good job – just one.'

It helped Mum's work with students that she was always up

to date in pop music, comedy and football. One of the cards she received from her pupils says: 'Thank you for making me understand the relationship of Dido and Aeneas with reference to the troubles of Sol Campbell at Arsenal.'[28]

School was also a good place for Mum to show her commitment to equality and her willingness to stand up to authority, first as the NUT representative at St Michael's Grammar School for Girls in the fiery strike days of the 1980s, then at the heart of an important equality case against the Corporation of London on behalf of fellow teachers at the City of London School for Girls.[29]

To quote a colleague, Gayle:

She was someone with an absolutely clear vision about the rights and wrongs of a case and was tenacious in arguing for what was right not just for the majority but also individuals, at some risk to herself. I, and I think most of us, had complete trust in her judgement. At

---

28 Amongst my brothers, I think I had the unique experience of being taught in school by my mum, being sent by the neighbouring boys' comprehensive to do my Latin A level at St Michael's Girls. Watching her teach was a revelation: the girls loved her, and even a truculent teenage eejit like me could see why – she'd bounce around the classroom making jokes, taking the mickey, imparting wisdom. She made Latin verse sing the way it was meant to be heard, just like the best teachers of Shakespeare.

29 It wasn't just fellow teachers Mum stood up for in the 1980s. In Margaret Thatcher's own constituency, where we lived, Mum went door to door, street by street, evening after evening, collecting clothes and tinned food for striking miners. I might have turned out a leftie anyway, but it was writ in stone from the time Mum made me read *The Ragged-Trousered Philanthropists*. She remained a staunch Labour supporter all her life, although I will always bitterly regret arguing instead of listening when she would tell me that it was going to cost Gordon Brown dear if he didn't do something about inheritance tax. But she never dreamed of saying 'I told you so' when that time came.

the same time, she was gentle and humorous. I can hear her characteristic laugh now. What an admirable person.

Mum could be disobedient to authority about less serious issues too. If you look at the photo on the back of your service, you may just see Mum in Hornsey Street with the Emirates Stadium in the background, celebrating a 5–2 win for Arsenal over Spurs in 2012.

What might not strike you at first is that in the shadow of a stadium from which 60,000 people have just left, she has virtually the whole street to herself.

This is because the police used to block that street off for no very good reason, and – tired of arguing the point every week – Mum came up with a dodge for us to get down the road. Thankfully the police have backed down and everyone can use the street now.

Mum showed the same fierce loyalty to Arsenal that she showed to any side she was on. Colleagues at City of London recall that she promised to dye her hair red if Arsenal won the Cup final in May 2002, and when Arsenal did their part, the redhead duly arrived for work on Monday.

As well as working as a teacher long beyond the normal retirement age, she was also went well beyond the normal retirement age for mums, running a sort of mission control for crisis management even after we'd all left home.

I remember her patiently tracking my progress down Africa from Finchley long before the days of the internet and email, and making sure in every country I passed through, there would be a package waiting at the General Post Office, sorting out my every need, along with her lovely letters and characteristic news-paper clippings of interest.

Even Prime Minister Gordon Brown knew that if he wanted to track down his missing adviser Damian on the weekends or evenings, the person to contact first was Barbara McBride.

As Mum got older, she revisited the things that had meant a lot to her: she bought a holiday flat in Nice which she kindly let many of us here today use; she attended Nelson Mandela's 80th birthday party in Parliament Square as a guest of the gov-ernment; she was invited to become a Freeperson of the City of London; she cried when she met John Carlos, one of the athletes who bravely gave the Black Power salute at the 1968 Olympics;[30] and Chris sorted out a trip to Italy so she could revisit the scenes of her favourite Classics lessons.

Of course, when ill health was diagnosed, there was a greater urgency to complete some circles of life. Mum revisited Kneb-worth House with her big sister, Rose. She went to Las Vegas to see Yvonne, her only childhood friend who'd moved away. And she contacted Chris's dad in Texas, and talked warmly about what had happened in both their lives since they'd parted.

Mum also said it was a silly thing but she could not live all her life in London without seeing its longest-running play, Agatha

---

[30] A few months before John Carlos and Tommie Smith became her heroes, she had lost another in Martin Luther King. 'Oh God, they've shot that lovely man!' she said when she picked up the paper on 5 April 1968. 'Who?' my brother Chris replied, 'Harold Wilson?'

Christie's *The Mousetrap*. Although I wish I hadn't asked her during the interval who she thought had done it, because as usual she was way ahead of me, and had already solved the mystery.

How did Mum live her life? Well, first I think she was a Christian not just in faith but in action. Her friend Karen wrote to me: 'She had a very gentle way with her, and had a compassion for the underdog or those less served.'

But a passage that resonated with me when I think about Mum comes from another teacher, in Alan Bennett's *The History Boys*, when he gives his advice to his pupils on how to live:

'Pass the parcel. Take it, feel it and pass it on. Not for me, not for you, but for someone, somewhere, one day. Pass it on, boys. That's the game I want you to learn. Pass it on.'

Well, as long as I knew her, Mum took her turn with the parcel to cram in as many gifts as she possibly could to pass to the next ones down the line.

So on behalf of her sons, thank you, our selfless, formidable, loving, magnificent Mum.

BARBARA MCBRIDE:
A EULOGY PART TWO

8 AUGUST 2014

Yesterday, we said goodbye to my mum, Barbara McBride.

Her service was at St Joseph's, Highgate, close to the nursing home where she died. She was buried down the road in Finchley, near to the family home where she spent most of her adult life. We managed to get her a plot in the same beautifully kept row where her own mum and dad rest, a spot she knew well from three decades of tending their grave.

She died just short of her seventy-seventh birthday, no age for a woman who kept fit and had no vices, unless we're counting the occasional sweet sherry, a Bailey's at Christmas, and a bet on *all* the Irish horses in the National. Instead, she fell victim to the non-BSE form of Creutzfeldt-Jakob Disease.

There are no good diseases, but I'd say CJD is right up there in the top ten bastards. It gradually took away every function Mum's mind controlled, except – cruelly – the awareness of everything that was happening to her, and the ensuing sense of pain, indignity, frustration and fear.

Even a few months ago – once she'd lost all speech, all mobility, and all but reflex functions – we could still see in her eyes that she knew what we were saying to her or what she was watching on TV, but had no means to express the thoughts in her head.

From what I could tell, even that awareness eventually waned in her final weeks, and after some hideous struggles with pneumonia and other infections, the end – when it came – was surprisingly swift and peaceful. Her weakened heart just stopped beating, and she drifted away in her sleep on the morning of 19 July.

Given the sad and shocking way her life ended, it's not surprising that my brothers and I have been hearing one message from all well-wishers this last fortnight and at yesterday's funeral service: focus on the good times; think of the happy memories; remember her the way she was.

That was certainly what my brother's beautiful eulogy at the service did, rightly hailing her as a firebrand for equality, a brilliant teacher, a scourge of authority, and the best mum anyone could wish for.

When I asked her why she always stayed up so late and got up so early, she replied that you might as well be dead if you stayed in bed all day, and that was the way she lived her life right up to the period that everyone has been urging us to forget, in preference for everything that went before, and the memories that we can happily celebrate.

And yet, and yet, just as Barbara displayed greatness in how she lived, in her roles as a teacher, a campaigner, a mother and a friend, I find myself needing also to acknowledge the greatness in how she died.

As the centenary commemorations of the First World War continue, we will marvel time and again at the courage of the men who went over the top into the barbed wire, machine guns and mustard gas, amongst them Barbara's granddad, killed at Étaples in December 1917.

But at least those men had their mates around them, the adrenalin of battle fuelling them, the prayer that maybe this time the bombardment had done its job, the hope that – if death came – at least it might be quick and painless, and the knowledge that – if they could just get through today – they'd be off the front line for weeks. And ultimately they had no choice.

Then I think about the courage my mum showed over these past two years. Knowing that she faced certain death, with no treatment possible. Knowing that there would not be good days and bad days, just ever worse days. And knowing that, with every month that passed, all the things that make life worth living would be gradually stripped away from her.

Yet she never succumbed to any despair or inertia, any bitterness or anger, whatever fresh blow she faced – from losing the ability to feed herself to losing the ability to swallow food full stop. A condition which is supposed to change your personality never seemed to affect hers, even when the only sign of it left was the look in her eyes.

It was true courage, displayed not instinctively in the heat of a moment, but day after day, month after month, until the day she died.

It was in keeping with her strong belief that people and institutions are defined not just by what they achieve, but by how they conduct themselves. She loved Arsenal and Middlesex all her life not for the trophies they won, but because they had a certain way of doing things.

When I was young, after I'd disgraced myself by refusing to give the 'three cheers' after we'd lost a primary school football match, I got a good hiding from my dad.

But my mum instead taught me Sir Henry Newbolt's poem 'Vitai Lampada', and explained to me that you were measured in life by playing the game with the same passion, effort, determination and good sportsmanship whether you were five goals up or five goals down.

The much misunderstood, unfairly maligned second verse of 'Vitai Lampada'[31] came back to me every time I visited her these past few months, and I read the poem at her Mass yesterday:

---

31 'Vitai Lampada' was derided after the First World War, for which it had initially been commandeered as a patriotic call to arms. Newbolt himself called it a Frankenstein's monster, appalled at how it had come to be regarded as symptomatic of a culture which treated war like a game, a great adventure, a jolly lark. Reading it now outside that context, it's clear the poem does nothing of the sort – it couldn't be a bleaker depiction of the realities of war, but it rightly argues that soldiers can find the courage to keep fighting in even the most dire circumstances, not by thinking about 'England' or 'Honour', but simply by remembering their own belief in 'playing the game' to the end.

The sand of the desert is sodden red, —
Red with the wreck of a square that broke; —
The Gatling's jammed and the Colonel dead,
And the regiment blind with dust and smoke.
The river of death has brimmed his banks,
And England's far, and Honour a name,
But the voice of a schoolboy rallies the ranks:
'Play up! Play up! And play the game!'

When facing certain death, with nothing and no one left to fight for, and only more pain and anguish left to look forward to, it takes special courage to keep fighting, to stay alive as long as possible, just because that is 'the game', and you always give your utmost right to the end, no matter how hard it is.

I don't think I have that courage, but when my time comes, I know I couldn't want for a better lesson than the one my mum has given.

And while I will always think first of the happy times and great achievements of Barbara's lifetime, I will also celebrate the fact that she died as she lived, conducting herself in a certain way: defiant and courageous; patient and selfless; a teacher and a fighter; an inspiring woman and an incredible mum.

Goodbye Babs, with all my love and thanks.

DON'T DISMISS ALAN BRAZIL...

12 AUGUST 2014

After the suicide of Robin Williams, TalkSport presenter Alan Brazil came under fire the following morning, when he said he had no sympathy for Williams and could not understand how he could leave his family in that way.

WHEN I PUBLISHED my book last year, I wrote that I discounted suicide as an option after my sacking from Downing Street because I could not 'do that' to my mum and my then girlfriend, given how much they were already suffering.

What I didn't say in the book was exactly how many nights

during that period I sat on my eighth-floor balcony pondering the drop into darkness below, or the enormous stash of prescription painkillers I keep in my flat, and – to fight the lure of how easy it would be – pondered instead how hard it would be on Balshen and Barbara.

I thought about that period recently given Balshen has now married someone else and my mum has recently died. Does that mean if I felt as hopelessly low tomorrow as I did back then in 2009 that I'd have no reason to stay alive? Or would I find new people to invest in now as my 'reasons' not to commit suicide?

But – even then – what on earth would it say about my mental condition if the best reason I can find to stay alive is how some other select people would feel if I wasn't?

This is why Alan Brazil must not be sacked by TalkSport, despite the furore over his 'no sympathy' exchanges on the radio today. That phrase may have been cruel but his comments overall cannot just be dismissed as ignorant. In fact, they're vitally important for all of us when discussing this terrible disease.

Focus for a moment on why Alan appeared to veer between obviously apathetic to quite angry about Robin Williams's apparent suicide: because – as he said – it is 'diabolical' to do that to your family, especially to any children.

How many times over the years have you heard someone say in public – in reaction to a Tannoy announcement of delays because of a 'passenger incident' – that they couldn't throw themselves under a Tube train because it would be 'selfish' to their fellow commuters and the poor Tube driver?

How many times have you heard people say in public – in reaction to the suicide of a famous person – that they couldn't do that themselves because of the impact on their spouse or their kids or their parents?

Then think how many people – how many millions of people of all ages – in our country are walking around in private for at least several days each year with deeply unhappy, borderline-suicidal thoughts, but thinking, 'I could never do that because of what it would do to X or Y.'

But in the worst cases, trying to convince yourself that other people are the only reason to stay alive is an express ticket to the funeral home. In a case like mine, because what do you do when they're gone? But in cases of serious depression, because the demon that tears at your heart and mind every day continually tells you that even those people would be better off (or wouldn't care) if you were dead, because the whole world would be better off (or wouldn't care) if you were dead, and by God, being dead would be so much better than another day of feeling like this.

When you get deep, deep down in that hole, the only thing that's going to stop you sinking further is finding a reason that you want to stay alive – for you. And once you've got that to hang onto, the only thing that's going to get you out of the hole is help. Including the help those lovely people you care about can give. But mainly professional help and drugs and a routine that allows you to take it all on board.

But if you ever find yourself contemplating suicide and the only thing stopping you is – as Alan Brazil bemoaned wasn't the case for Robin Williams – your loved ones, then that's good for today, but you are still in very serious trouble, and you need to get professional help.

The best thing Alan Brazil could do tonight is acknowledge that, and admit he cannot comprehend what it is like when even the thought of your daughter's reaction cannot prevent the attraction of the abyss, and that he has immense sympathy for anyone who ever reaches that terrible low.

RIP Robin Williams: good game, Bob.

HAPPY 40TH BIRTHDAY, SHIV

16 AUGUST 2014

I'VE HAD JUST two real sporting heroes in my life.

The first was Paul Davis, the silk in the steel of Arsenal's trophy-winning sides of the George Graham era. I loved Davo from his emergence in the early 1980s through to his crowning glory, the Cup Winners' Cup final in 1994. But I'll write about him another day.

Just a fortnight or so before Arsenal's triumph in Copenhagen, I found my second sporting hero, even if I didn't know it at the time.

While the cricketing world was transfixed by Brian Lara's attempt to beat Gary Sobers's world record for the highest Test innings, my eye was increasingly drawn to the nineteen-year-old at the other end, Shivnarine Chanderpaul.

In only his first international series, the young Guyanese had the maturity and tenacity to hold his end up during a four-and-a-half-hour partnership of 219 runs, ensuring Lara could break the record without having to bat with the unreliable West Indies tail.

I remember thinking how unjust it was that West Indies declared as soon as Lara was out, rather than allowing his partner to dash for the twenty-five more runs he needed for his maiden century. As it was, Shiv achieved what would prove to be a different milestone: the first 'not out' score of his Test career.

Nobody realised it during that 1994 series against England, but just as Chanderpaul's career was beginning, the golden age of West Indies cricket was starting to end. Top of the ICC test rankings until August 1995, they are now stuck in a distant eighth, and have been for most of the last decade.

For those of us who have stayed with the team and suffered through that decline, there have been many terrible lows, some moments of utter farce and incredulity, and – almost as crushing – the multiple false dawns; hopes raised and dashed in the space of a session.

But then there has been Shiv. The only connection back to that golden age. The only rock of stability during two decades of turmoil.

Usually coming to the crease at No. 4 or 5 with the innings in crisis, he hammers a bail into the pitch with the handle of his bat to mark his guard, fidgets with his gloves, blinks, pulls at his shirt, licks at an imaginary ice cream, then stands face-on to the bowler, his stumps exposed, bat aloft.

The delivery comes and he shuffles sideways across his stumps, always leaving the stroke as late as possible, always played with soft hands, seemingly able to carve the ball in any direction he chooses; a cricketer who uses his bat like a table tennis paddle.

The ball is survived, and the routine begins again – blinking, fidgeting, licking, staring down the wicket, intensely concentrating on surviving the next ball. And the next. And the next. Nobody in the history of Test cricket – not even Geoff Boycott – has prized their wicket as highly as Shiv.

If, once in your career, you batted for more than 1,000 minutes – almost seventeen hours – without getting out, usually over the course of three or four separate innings, you'd have achieved something pretty remarkable. Boycott never managed it. Sachin Tendulkar, Jacques Kallis and Rahul Dravid did it once each.

Shiv has achieved that feat four times; on one occasion spending a world record twenty-five hours at the crease between dismissals.[32]

This could cause me one or two problems work-wise. When I was working in the Treasury, I could happily have the West Indies on the telly in my office, but in the open-plan spaces inside Downing Street, this was harder to get away with, especially when Gordon could walk in at any time.

So I'd tend to wait until the internet told me Shiv was batting,

---

32 If that makes Shiv sound like a steady accumulator of runs in the Rahul Dravid mode, don't forget he can bang as well when the game demands it. His 69-ball Test century against Australia in 2003 is the joint fourth fastest of all time, and his ten off two balls to clinch a one-day victory against Sri Lanka is one of my happiest sporting memories. Ian Bishop: 'Has it gone? Has it gone? Has it gone? Has it gone? It's gone!!!!'

then hotfoot it up to Haymarket to watch him in the Sports Café. I'd tell myself I'll just stay here until Shiv gets out ... and six hours later, I'd still be there.

If you want to see that determination in action, take a look at this incident from Australia's 2008 tour: Brett Lee appears to knock Shiv unconscious with a bouncer. Shiv not only got up and resumed his innings, but went on to make 118. Over the next two Tests, he recorded the most recent of his four 1,000-minute unbeaten spells, this in the course of a 2–0 series defeat.

Because what do you do when you are one of the highest-ranked batsmen in the world, playing for a side officially ranked the worst of the major Test-playing nations?

What *can* you do other than continue playing to the best of your ability, setting yourself personal challenges, adding to your records of fifties and centuries, keeping your average up, chasing the next target on the list of all-time run-scorers, and above all, not getting out?

As a result, Shiv has occasionally faced accusations – including, without irony, from Kevin Pietersen – of putting his own interests before the team's. 'Why doesn't he bat higher in the order?', they say. 'Why doesn't he nurse the strike when batting with the tail?'

By their reckoning, Shiv's joint world record of 46 not-out innings for a top-order batsman is a sign of failure not of success, rather ignoring the fact that he currently shares the record with the ultimate team-player, Steve Waugh.

As a now long-suffering West Indies fan, I can tell you any criticism of Shiv on these grounds is utter baloney. On the frequent occasions I find myself screaming at the television while watching them, it's not 'Why didn't you come in at No. 3 instead, Shiv?' I'm shouting; it's 'For fuck's sake, Bravo, what kind of shot is that? Why can't you play like Shiv?'[33]

Many times over the last twenty years, I've wondered why I put myself through the wringer with the West Indies, why I force myself to follow every doomed series and invest hope in every new player. It would be so much easier to give up and invest my energy and emotions into something more rewarding.

But it's not just that Shiv is always what draws me back; it's that I look at him applying himself with the same dedication and resolve each innings, no matter how hopeless the cause or how reckless his fellow batsmen, and I think: well, if he can stick it out, the least you can do is stick with him.

And the reality is the West Indies should have built their team around Shiv this last decade. At the very least, every other batsman coming into the team in that period should have been instructed to model their approach to the game on his, instead of all trying to be the next Brian Lara or Chris Gayle.

There are some signs of hope. Notably, young opener Kraigg Brathwaite looks like a chip off Shiv's block, and the captaincy of the team – which never sat well with Shiv during his own spell as skipper – appears to be turning Denesh Ramdin into a more responsible player.

---

33 I'm not picking on Darren Bravo specifically, although he is a serial offender for irresponsible dismissals brought on by a lack of concentration, especially for such a talented player. But you could equally replace his name with the likes of Edwards, Powell, Simmons, Gayle, Smith etc. etc.

And Shiv himself looks as hungry as ever for more runs and new records. It's been twenty years since a man over the age of forty made a Test century (Graham Gooch), and only one West Indian – Clive Lloyd – has ever achieved the feat. Next month's tour by Bangladesh offers the ideal opportunity.

I'll be watching every second. After all, who knows how many more Test series my hero will carry on for? He's been a huge part of my life for twenty years, and now it's time to savour every innings, concentrate on every ball and enjoy every run as if it could be his last.

A bit like the man himself.

Happy birthday, Shiv.

Chanderpaul did indeed go on to make a century against Bangladesh, and was not out in all three of his innings in the two-match series, batting unbeaten for 743 minutes.

FERGUSON TODAY VERSUS NEW YORK FIFTY YEARS AGO

18 AUGUST 2014

MANY PEOPLE HAVE already pointed out the parallels between events in Ferguson, Missouri over the past week, and the successive outbreaks of rioting in Harlem and Rochester, New York, fifty years ago in July.

Both riots have echoes in the Ferguson crisis. The Harlem riot was caused when a fifteen-year-old was shot dead in the street by an off-duty police officer. In Rochester, it was rumoured police brutality in the arrest of a nineteen-year-old during a block party.

In both cases, the individual incidents were the catalysts for out breaks of violent protests, highly selective looting and heavy-handed police responses, played out over several days.

I've gone back to the Master's dissertation I wrote twenty years ago about urban rioting to dig out some quotes from individuals who participated in and responded to those 1964 New York riots, along with excerpts from my own analysis. For those who ask how much has changed over the past fifty years, the following quotes will make interesting reading:

New York Times editorial, 23 April 1964:

> The war here will not be won until social and economic inequities are as dead as legal ones. The primary and fundamental requisites in this city are better housing, education, job opportunities and an unequivocal willingness on the part of taxpayers and citizens to provide all three, no matter what the cost.

Man speaking at a Congress of Racial Equality (CORE) rally before the Harlem riots, quoted in *Newsweek*, 3 August 1964:

> It is time to let The Man know that if he does something to us, we are going to do something back. Then we might get some respect.

'Man, aged about thirty-three', quoted in K. B. Clark, *Dark Ghetto*, 1965:

> We really don't need cops here in Harlem. They start more

violence than [anyone]. Here comes a cop: 'You're disturbing the peace!', he says. No one has made a complaint. Everyone is enjoying themselves. But one cop'll want to chase everyone.

'A middle-aged barber', quoted in K. B. Clark, op. cit.:

I ain't sayin' I like what these kids are doin', but I don't dislike it either. They gettin' more action than all the rest of them put together. Nobody ever thinks about Harlem until something like this happens.

K. B. Clark, quoted in *Newsweek*, op. cit.:

The horrible living conditions ... apparently no one gives a damn about. They send thousands of cops. They would do better to send half as many building inspectors or a thousand sanitation workers or just an attempt at proper schooling.

K. B. Clark, quoted in the *New York Times*, 22 July 1964:

I've walked the streets of Harlem the last two days and I have heard Negroes saying, 'We've got nothing to lose. What more can happen?' I don't know how the average Civil Rights leader can ask his race to be moderate anymore.

Judy Howell, CORE's Bronx youth coordinator, quoted in I. F. Stone, *In a Time of Torment*, 1965:

Maybe we'd better have a riot here too. Those people downtown
didn't have a dime for young people 'til the riots broke out in
Harlem. Now the churches have come up with $100,000 and
the city with $200,000. We here in the Bronx have managed
with $60 so far this summer.

Me, citing Jay Schulman's analysis: 'Ghetto-area residence, political alienation, riot orientation', 1968:

> Whereas riot participants were dismissed as the 'riff-raff' of the
> black community, already predisposed towards violence and
> robbery, in Rochester it was the poorest and most delinquent
> teenagers (along with transient Southern migrants) who were
> consistently found to be apathetic or ill-disposed towards rioting.
> While 80 per cent of the black population described themselves
> as unopposed to the use of riots as an 'instrument of social
> change', the most favourable respondents were the most aspir-
> ant, least deprived members of the ghetto community.

Harry McPherson,[34] LBJ's chief of staff, quoted in *Chief of
Staff: Twenty-Five Years of Managing the Presidency*, Kernell and
Popkin, 1986:

---

34 While recorded three years after the 1964 riots, it's interesting – in light of events in Ferguson – to
note this anecdote from Harry McPherson in a memo to President Johnson, written on 8 August 1967:

*It was hot. A few men were sitting on the kerb, talking. A cop in a patrol car said: 'Get up off that
kerb!' The Negroes didn't move. There was a lot of low cursing. Achievement: bad feelings, ineffective
enforcement of the law. Two strikes for disorder later on.*

There was a grinding inexorability to events. People who had long been suppressed, through a whole concatenation of political and demographic events, suddenly just [rioted].

Me, citing his interview in Kernell and Popkin, op cit.:

Harry McPherson's fact-finding trip to [New York] produced a damning indictment of unemployment; terrible housing and streets; rats; and abusive, corrupt and almost exclusively white policing as the conditions working for the occurrence of a riot, as opposed to agitators, who 'have a hard time raising a crowd'.

White House memo: Norbert Schlei to Lee White, 3 September 1964:

The common denominator [in the 1964 riots] is the existence of a disenchanted segment of the population living under the most unsatisfactory conditions and disaffected from society ... particularly young men. Problems of urban life: unemployment, poverty, inadequate housing and education, and juvenile delinquency have tended to be magnified by racial discrimination.

Internal White House policy document, entitled 'Riots and Crime in the Cities', September 1964:

Obviously the basic ills which caused the riots are not susceptible of immediate cure. But it should be axiomatic that any attempt to remedy them be taken in an atmosphere in which law and order are preserved.

Lyndon Baines Johnson, *The Vantage Point: Perspectives on the Presidency, 1963–69*, 1971:

> No one could have predicted the scope of the problems that the [1964] riots represented, but it was clear they foreshadowed dark days ahead. I believed the real danger, far more profound and far more perilous, was the increasing alienation of black citizens from American society. As long as these citizens were alienated from the rights of the American system, they would continue to consider themselves outside the obligations of that system.

MEASURES THAT MAKE
YOU GO 'HMMM'...

1 SEPTEMBER 2014

MY FIRST JOB in government, almost twenty years ago now, was working for HM Customs & Excise, in its anti-smuggling policy department. We were responsible for the smuggling of drugs, tobacco, booze, fuel, endangered species, indecent and obscene material, and firearms.

Because the IRA were involved in some of those trades, there was a big overlap with the anti-terrorism work of the security forces too. And, over time, anti-smuggling operations also became subsumed in the work of the various agencies set up to tackle organised crime.

Maybe things have changed since then, but my memory is that

there was very little we didn't know about passengers travelling on different aircraft, or – put another way – there was very little information the airlines had that wasn't shared with us, either formally or informally.

We'd know the name and details of each passenger according to their passport, how and where they'd bought their ticket (and, crucially, who had paid for that ticket), who they were travelling with, what route they were travelling, how many bags they were taking out with them and – where they'd been loaded into the hold – how much those bags weighed. And so on.

When those passengers returned, it was therefore relatively easy to spot where something suspicious was going on: they were travelling back with someone different; they'd changed their route; they were carrying more bags than they'd taken out, or their bags were now fully laden. On occasion, you'd then take a wee (not strictly legal) peek in their hold luggage before it went on the conveyor belt to check whether you were right to be suspicious.

That was all very productive work, but it's worth pointing out that if you were reliant on that analysis of passenger manifest information to identify all your suspects, let alone taking a sneaky shufty in their bags, it would be a pretty seat-of-the-pants operation.

By a long distance, the majority of our potential suspects were instead identified in advance via intelligence sources, surveillance work etc. both in the UK and overseas. In other words, the red flags were waving long before those suspects ever checked onto a plane.

So I find myself puzzled and intrigued by the headlines saying that David Cameron will today ask airlines to increase the information they provide about their passengers, and that the government believes this will be a significant addition to their armoury of weapons against the jihadists.

And let's be clear: that is *the* headline measure from today's package of anti-terror powers, so you'd expect it to be significant.

I'll suspend judgement until I see all the details, or hear from some of the security talking heads, but in the meantime, I'm prepared to whisper a provisional call of 'bullshit' against this measure.

First, I'm not convinced there's much useful information the airlines can give the authorities beyond what they already provide. And second, if our security services are genuinely reliant on that extra passenger information to identify potential terror suspects, then we'd better raise the 'threat level' to 'Run!'

If I'm right, that would rather suggest that – after a weekend of frantic negotiations and civil service barrel-scraping – the government's been reduced to this nonsense just so it's got something to say to match the wildly overblown rhetoric from the PM on Friday.

Yet another example of David Cameron adopting a solution before bothering to examine the problem.

WHY MY DAD
WOULD BE
VOTING 'NO'

17 SEPTEMBER 2014

MY DAD WAS the proudest Scot you'd ever meet.

Eugene McBride was born near Gorbals Cross in Glasgow in January 1937. His earliest memory was watching the skyline lit up from the tenement window as the Luftwaffe bombed Clydebank four years later.

His father took the family back to their native Donegal to see out the war, but my dad eventually returned to see out his schooling, and start his lifelong love affair with Glasgow Celtic.[35] After a spell in the seminary, he came down to London as a student, met my mum, fell in love, got married, started our family, and that was him stuck down south, except for his pilgrimages back to Parkhead, usually wrapped around a long weekend staying with his childhood friend John Butterly MBE.

Being Scottish was just part of growing up in our house in London. I'm fairly sure I was the only kid in my primary school class who celebrated Burns Night and stopped watching the World Cup after the first round.[36]

Chic Murray and Billy Connolly were our favourite comedians; *Gregory's Girl* and *Local Hero* our favourite films; and no evening was complete without the sound of marching pipes and drums booming from my dad's record player. Not because all that entertainment was Scottish in origin, but because it was the best.

Never one to back down, Eugene would regularly get into heated swearing matches with people on the street and in shops who made racist jibes at him. I'd genuinely wonder how they knew he was

---

35 Trying to reconcile the feelings of being both Scottish and British is relatively easy, compared to the tortured knots faced by anyone who – like my dad and me – feels simultaneously Scottish, British and Irish, especially trying to sort out where to lay the blame for the past 500 years of tyranny. Pinning it all on 'cruel England' – as Dominic Behan would have it – is something of a mug's game given the role that Scottish settlers and rich Irish landowners played. It's no wonder some people retreat into a rather simpler sectarian divide, but my dad would never have any of that. He would just tell me: 'It's complicated.' Quite so.

36 A Scotland victory over England in the Home Internationals was always a cause of huge celebration; a defeat and my dad's resulting temper was a thing to be feared. Which made it all the more memorable when he came home from Wembley after one defeat (I think in 1983), and greeted my commiserations by saying sorrowfully that he'd ended up hoping England would win because of the monkey noises being made at Luther Blissett by a section of Scotland fans.

Scottish; it never occurred to me that he had a strong Glaswegian accent – to me he just sounded like my dad.

I got a decent education about the Highland Clearances and other atrocities just listening to those rows, and no long walk with Eugene was ever complete without an impromptu lecture on Scottish history, culture and football.

But of all the stories he ever told me – of all the things that he clearly enjoyed retelling (other than Chic Murray jokes) – none would recur so frequently as the heroism of the Highland Division at El Alamein, and the tears in the eyes of all who saw the survivors march in victory through Tripoli three months later.

(If you want to get a sense of what that would have been like, watch their parade in Germany in 1945.)

Those soldiers helped turn the battle in the battle that helped turn the war, and my dad would weep with pride when he told me what those brave men had done on behalf of Scotland, Britain, and the free world.

It was the same feeling that would put tears in his eyes when Alan Wells won in Moscow or Liz McColgan won in Tokyo: proud Scots doing it for Britain. It was the same feeling he'd have when reminding any young Liverpool or Man United fans that Celtic were the first British club to win the European Cup.

His pride was always at its peak when Scotland showed it was the best of Britain, not when it showed its back to Britain.

So if he was still alive and living back in Glasgow, with a vote to cast in tomorrow's referendum, I would bet that he'd think of Clydebank, El Alamein and Lisbon, and calmly put his cross against 'No'.

And if any of the 'Yes' campaign mobs dared call him a 'traitor', an 'Uncle Tom' or a 'slave' for doing so, then I'd wish them best of luck in the swearing match to follow.

ENGLISH VOTES FOR
ENGLISH LAWS ... MEH

19 SEPTEMBER 2014

H OW PLEASANTLY TYPICAL of the United Kingdom...
Come on, at the first use of the words 'United Kingdom', you're now supposed to cheer; just like you do at a
wedding the first time the groom mentions his 'wife'.

OK, I'll start again.

How pleasantly, typically British that a political class which
only a few hours ago was panicking at the prospect of the Union
breaking apart is now getting ready to tear itself to bits over what
the expected victory of the 'No' campaign means for poor old

England, and engaging in dreadful revisionism over whether the threat from the 'Yes' campaign was ever that big after all.

Now we face the abysmal prospect of David Cameron making some speech about the future of England which he thinks is so serious and urgent that it has to be made at seven in the morning – in time for the markets opening – as if he was the M&S chairman announcing a moth infestation at the pants warehouse.

Over the coming days, there will be lots of talk of creating an English Parliament, which will dissipate as soon as anyone points out the cost. Tory MPs will demand the scrapping of the Barnett Formula or Gordon Brown's package of extra devolved powers, neither of which will be countenanced given the 'Vow' signed by all three English party leaders before yesterday's referendum.

So the inevitable upshot of all this kerfuffle will simply be the long-heralded introduction of 'English Votes for English Laws', i.e. Scottish, Welsh and Northern Irish MPs being barred from voting on Westminster legislation that does not affect their constituencies.

Obviously, there will be all sorts of problems with this, but, like it or not, that's where we're going to end up. And – at the risk of seeming a little carefree given my giddiness at the United Kingdom's survival – here's my question: what does it matter?

From a Labour point of view especially, what does it really matter?

Let's assume the worst-case scenario where a Labour government (or coalition) owes its majority (or its largest-party status) to its Scottish MPs, but does not have a majority (even in coalition) when it comes to English votes.

It can happily rely on its overall majority to pass its Budget legislation on taxes and other fiscal matters; it can legislate for increases in the minimum wage or reductions in the retirement age; it can take the country to war or get agreement on international treaties; it can approve major spending or infrastructure projects which affect the whole of the UK; and it can introduce new or tighter laws to protect our national security.

So what else is there? Legislation affecting our schools, NHS, transport network, and so on, obviously. 'The last Labour government couldn't have introduced tuition fees without Scottish votes!', I hear you cry. Well, without reopening those old scars, is it a terrible thing that anything a future Labour government does to our NHS, schools or other England-only public services should be capable of commanding a parliamentary consensus?

When I think of the vast gamut of reforms and improvements that Andy Burnham, Yvette Cooper, Tristram Hunt, Mary Creagh and others might be planning to introduce in the next parliament, I'm not convinced that they include a whole series of controversial laws waiting to be blocked by that putative English Tory majority. Not unless the Tories just want to block things for the sake of blocking things, and look like total dicks in the process.

Maybe I'm being naive, but – as earth-shattering as EV4EL sounds in theory – I just don't think it will end up being that much of a big deal. In which case, David Cameron can get up as early as he likes to make his ridiculous dawn speech with his big serious face on, but the rest of us should just stay in bed, have a lie-in, and bask in the fact that we are still one United Kingdom.

For which, thank you, Gordon.

And God bless the Queen.

ED BALLS:
A LOT OF TOUGH TACKLES;
A FEW SUBTLE PASSES

22 SEPTEMBER 2014

E D BALLS'S PREVIOUS conference speeches as shadow Chancellor have evoked Labour's generation of 1945: the Attlee government rebuilding from the rubble, paying down large national debts but not allowing that to dim their big ambitions.

Today's speech echoed a different period in Labour history before an equally momentous victory: Labour's Clause 4 conference in Brighton twenty years ago, and the rigid fiscal authority and discipline enforced by Gordon Brown in the run-up to the

1997 election, including very clearly setting out what Labour's first Budget would do and, by extension, what it would not.

That had the conference cheering, as did earlier passages on the NHS, but bar a couple of jokes and a few brief moments which tugged at the heartstrings – the lad in his constituency on a zero-hours contract and Balls's mention of his own stammer – the message was uncompromisingly, unremittingly tough.

On top of things we've heard previously like the mansion tax and compulsory jobs guarantee, we had the new pledge to cut child benefit in real terms until 2017, the prospect of earlier increases in the retirement age, warnings of further public sector pay restraint in the next parliament and yet more clamping down on hedge funds and the tax avoidance industry.

Balls also coupled the restatement of Labour's new fiscal rules with a pledge that there will be no unfunded and unaffordable tax or spending commitments in the manifesto. Contrast that with just two years ago, when he was happy to make the case for funding a VAT cut out of additional borrowing.

The pledge to undertake a zero-based review of public spending was also made again, and if David Cameron was watching, perhaps he should note that Ed Balls is rather happy to draw public attention to his tough old ZBR, so Dave should probably stop mentioning it all the time in PMQs as though it's some big secret Balls is hiding.

All in all, it was tough as old boots, so when we got to the 'I am tough but I am also fair' section – abolishing the bedroom tax, restoring the 10 pence income tax band etc. – I'm sure many in the conference hall felt like Rob Merrick in yesterday's football match, being offered a handshake and a tissue to stem the bleeding, and accepting both with a rather dazed smile.

Amidst all of the hard tackling, and lots more sturdy passages of play on jobs and skills, Europe, devolution to the regions etc., there were four other subtle, Mesut Ozil-style through-balls that caught my eye:

1. Last conference, Balls caused all sorts of ructions by appearing to go cautious on HS2. The rail project went totally unmentioned in this year's speech, unless you read between the lines of his insistence that his new independent National Infrastructure Commission will be charged with ensuring value for money in its recommendations. Will HS2 pass that test? Or will it be deemed an awful lot of bucks for very little bang?;

2. Balls also seemed to come as close as anyone has so far to saying Labour will accept Howard Davies's recommendation on airport capacity in the south-east, whatever it is. If Davies opts for expansion at Heathrow, that will be a pretty hard pill for Ed Miliband to swallow given his public opposition to a third runway both in government and during his leadership bid. But swallow it he should: it's not a U-turn, it's just growing up;

3. As the Tories are fond of reminding us, the revenues that

will be raised from a mansion tax have already been spent more times than Brewster's millions. But to be fair, Labour have simply changed their mind as time has passed on what the *priority* should be for spending those revenues, and last time I looked, the current priority was the reintroduction of the 10 pence income tax band. But today we learn that the 10 pence policy will instead be paid for by abolishing Cameron's cherished marriage tax break, neatly demolished by Balls in his speech. So how is the mansion tax money now going to be spent?; and

4. Balls has said similar things before, but as we get closer to George Osborne's pre-election budget, it's notable how his Labour counterpart remains committed to using the proceeds of selling the RBS and Lloyds shares to pay down the national debt instead of spending them on 'frivolous' pre-election giveaways. Osborne loves setting traps for Labour, but this is the big trap Balls is laying for him: how can Osborne make deficit reduction an election dividing line if he's on the wrong side of decisions like this?

Because, in conclusion, this wasn't a speech attempting to win the impending election by throwing around reckless promises to spend money that doesn't exist, like Osborne's conference speech before The Election That Never Was in 2007. In many ways, it was much bolder – and certainly much braver – than that.

It was saying to the British people: you want grown-up, tough, serious government? You want a Labour Party that's learnt from its mistakes? Well, this is what it looks like.

Now to see if they'll vote for it.

AN IMPORTANT DAY
FOR OUR MEDIA

28 SEPTEMBER 2014

AMID ALL THE media furore about Ed Miliband forgetting to mention the deficit in his speech last Tuesday, I observed to one journalist pal that his colleagues' renewed focus on the deficit issue was a double-edged sword for George Osborne, especially after Ed Balls's vow the previous day that Labour would make no tax or spending pledges funded from additional borrowing.

I said:

Osborne can hardly come out in his conference speech now or

> his pre-election Budget and say: 'Here's a big tax cut, but don't
> worry where the money's coming from, we'll find it somewhere.'
> After this week, the media can't let him get away with that, or
> they'll look like hypocrites.

I may have spoken too soon. I haven't seen all the coverage of Osborne's £150 million tax cut for individuals with pension pots invested in shares, but – as far as I can tell – only the *Daily Mail* has even asked the question 'How is this going to be paid for?', receiving the laughable answer that we will have to wait until the Autumn Statement to be told.

If Labour had last week made a pledge on tax or spending and been unable to say right away where the money was coming from to pay for it, that failure – on top of Ed Miliband's forgetfulness – would rightly have seen them slaughtered by the media for a lack of seriousness about getting the deficit down.

On that basis, George Osborne simply cannot be allowed to get away with doing the same thing, especially if tomorrow's pensions measure is just the first in a series of similarly unfunded announcements in his or Cameron's speeches this week, or in the Autumn Statement and Budget to come.

This is especially important because we are now in the territory of tax revenue permanently forgone. When poor Chloe Smith struggled to explain where the money would be found simply to defer a fuel duty increase for six months back in 2012, it was at least plausible that some departmental underspends could plug the temporary hole in tax revenues, thereby not requiring any more borrowing.

But tomorrow's £150 million tax cut is not a temporary measure: it requires the Treasury to raise another tax, or to permanently cut an area of spending, or to fund the measure through increased borrowing. The same will be true of any other substantial and permanent tax or spending measure we hear about this week or over the coming months.

If George Osborne is able to get away tomorrow without explaining in detail which of those options it will be, and how – if it is the latter – that squares with his commitments on the deficit, then the British media will be seriously failing in their duties. They must hold Osborne to the same standards they held Labour to last week.

THE HUMILITY HOLE
IN CAMERON'S SPEECH

2 OCTOBER 2014

'I DON'T CLAIM TO be a perfect leader,' David Cameron said yesterday. Really? After that speech, you could have fooled me.

If the deficit was the missing word in Ed Miliband's speech, the huge hole in this Tory conference has been any sense of humility, any acknowledgement whatsoever that some things have not gone to plan these past four years.

Indeed, the only time Cameron used the word 'mistakes' in his speech was to deride Ed Balls (with his irksome faux-indignation) for admitting that Labour had made some during its time in office.

Some of this is down to plain arrogance and bravado,[37] as per the astonishing hypocrisy and chutzpah with which Cameron and Osborne announced £8 billion in tax cuts and £22 billion in spending cuts without even the promise of an explanation as to where the money would be found.

But if they truly believe they can 'trade on their record' in convincing the public to accept those unfunded promises and unspecified savings at face value, they do themselves no favours by pretending that record is unblemished. Indeed, reinforcing the impression that they are arrogant, aloof and out of touch is the last thing they can afford.

When Tony Blair made his own pitch for a second term in office in late September 2000, he'd gone from a net satisfaction rating of zero to minus 30 in the space of a month, following the late summer fuel crisis.[38]

---

37 If you want another illustration of the casual arrogance of Cameron's speech, look no further than this line: 'I didn't come into politics to make the lines on the graphs go in the right direction.' That is a spectacularly stupid thing to say at any time, but with the highly fragile state of global stock markets and currency values, it is one colossal hostage to fortune.

38 In the run-up to the conference, John Rentoul suggested that David Cameron study Blair's 2000 speech, as well as Margaret Thatcher's in 1982. Thatcher was in the opposite situation to Blair, coming into that conference with her net satisfaction ratings just above zero from a low of minus 40 the year before, all via a large but short-lived spike in support during the Falklands War. For that reason, Thatcher perhaps didn't feel the need to acknowledge too many mistakes either, but it's interesting to note her respectful tone when appealing to Labour voters disillusioned by the party's commitment to unilateral nuclear disarmament. Contrast that with David Cameron yesterday, who – clearly having learnt nothing from his 'loonies and fruitcakes' description of UKIP voters – described voting Labour as the definition of madness. Incidentally, it's also fascinating to read Thatcher's words on Europe, in the face of Labour's internal battle on continued membership of the Single Market:

Those who would pull us out of Europe must come to terms with the damage that that would do to our people. Even the threat of withdrawal destroys jobs. Firms that invest in the Common Market often decide to come to Britain. Labour's threat to withdraw makes companies hesitate and look elsewhere. That Labour threat is losing us jobs now.

That Blair speech fourteen years ago gave nothing away to Cameron's yesterday in terms of passion, leadership, conviction and content, albeit Blair was berating William Hague's Tories for promising pie-in-the-sky tax and spending cuts, rather than announcing his own.

But, more importantly, Blair both acknowledged and took responsibility for what Labour had got wrong in the previous four years: the Dome; the 75p pension increase; the fuel crisis.

'There are things we have done that have made people angry and we should be open enough to admit it.'

By the end of the year, Blair had recovered almost all of the ground he'd lost that summer in his performance ratings. If that suggests public opinion was quite volatile in that period, David Cameron has the opposite problem: in two and a half years since the 2012 Omnishambles Budget, his ratings have hardly changed, bobbing around between minus 15 and minus 20.

That is a large wedge of the public who think he has made mistakes and do not believe he is doing his job well, but Cameron's reaction is not to address those opinions directly or acknowledge where they might have a point, in the way that Blair did.

Instead, he chose yesterday to throw tax promises, spending cuts, welfare blitzes, apprenticeships and new houses in the direction of his public critics, and hoped that – plus some Miliband-bashing and NHS-salivating – would do the trick.

And for all the fawning headlines and leader columns in response today, I'd say to David Cameron that his strategy is fundamentally flawed.

To hear all your promises, people first have to be listening. To get them both to listen and to believe you, you have to earn some respect and show you've listened to them. And you will never earn people's respect if you act as though the last four years have been some golden period in Britain's governmental history which we've all been blessed to live through, gawd bless you, sir.

A politician whom the public consider a good egg and an authentic person is gold-dust these days, but sadly as rare as unicorn droppings. The Tories have inexplicably said goodbye to William Hague, one of their few assets in that regard; Labour need Alan Johnson back on board, definitely one of theirs.

But humility is no bad proxy for authenticity: a politician who's prepared to admit their failings, accept their mistakes and be open about the difficulty of getting everything right goes a long way to opening up the ears of their audience when they go on to talk about what they're trying to achieve.

David Cameron's speech has been much praised today, but it was missing that vital section where he accepted that many of his government's decisions had made people angry, that they'd been unable to keep some of their promises, and that he was sorry to anyone who felt let down.

Indeed, his attack on Ed Miliband would have had much greater force if he'd said how hard he personally had found the job of being Prime Minister, how much he'd learnt from his mistakes, and how the experience he'd gained made him the right man to lead the country for the next five years.

Right now, assuming Nick Clegg's 2012 *mea culpa* on tuition fees was a one-off, Labour is the only party – and Ed Miliband the only leader – making a virtue of apologising for past mistakes, acknowledging the lessons learned, admitting that public trust must be regained, and – albeit in the shape of Miliband's ill-fated 'job interview' rhetoric – asking for a fresh start.

People might say 'about time too', or 'they need to go much further'. And that may be fair enough. But I'd far rather that was the criticism than the one that can rightly be levelled at David Cameron after yesterday's speech: he *does* think he's a perfect leader and doesn't think he's got anything wrong.

As long as Cameron keeps up that front, people's televisions will stay muted, and all his fine words and unfunded promises will float into the ether, like the hot air they are.

ACKNOWLEDGEMENTS

THANKS TO EVERYONE at Biteback Publishing for their assistance with this book, especially James Stephens for the initiative and Olivia Beattie for the editing.

Thanks to Jonathan Freedland, for his great patience during a woeful episode of false memory syndrome on my original edition of the article on 'The Election That Never Was'.

Thanks also to Jonathan, and to – amongst others – Ben Brogan, Michael Crick, Matthew D'Ancona, Tony Gallagher, Dan Hodges, Iain Martin, John McTernan, Tim Montgomerie, Vincent Moss, Fraser Nelson, John Rentoul, Steve Richards, Tim Shipman, Simon Walters, Zoe Williams, Paul Waugh, and of course Iain Dale and Lord Ashcroft, for providing much-valued words of encouragement during the early days of my blogging.

Finally, thanks above all to my literary consigliere Paula: the only person to read any of these articles before they were published, and whose thumbs-ups were always my personal Pulitzer Prize.

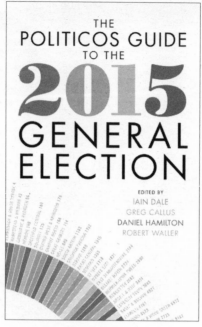

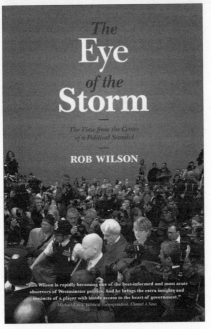

7-16(20)
12-20(23)

APR 1 2 2006

Also by Richard North Patterson

EYES OF A CHILD
DEGREE OF GUILT